My friend, Dr. Gary Carver is tl
insights, and inspiration cast a wide .
and community to every community of faith.

A distinguished scholar, pastor, and most of all friend, Gary is also the teacher's teacher. His decades-long "Got A Minute" series became a visionary precursor to the podcasts of our day and I am confident that the collection of stories and insights found in these pages will life our spirits in these most challenging days.

Rabbi Ken Kanter
Rabbinical Director,
Roots of Reform Judaism

Outstanding! I wholeheartedly recommend this collection of one minute stories to every pastor and regular speakers

Rear Admiral Vance H. Fry
U. S. Navy (Ret.)

"Gotta Minute" was the most uplifting and inspirational radio vignette I had ever heard. Now here it is in print for the world to read, enjoy and be inspired. Dr. Carver's "Gotta Minute" that is all it takes.

Johnny Eagle,
Aka Harold Loyd
Former General Manager
WFLI Radio
Chattanooga, Tennessee

I am a not native to Chattanooga, coming here as the successor to Dr. Carver at First Cumberland Presbyterian Church. As such, I never had the opportunity to hear him deliver his signature "Gotta Minute" on the Chattanooga airwaves. I am so thankful that he is now providing us with this wonderful collection of stories and reflections of hope and life. In reading this book, I feel like the Rev. Edward Everett who delivered a two hour address just before Abraham Lincoln's two minute Gettysburg Address. Everett wrote the president the next day saying, "I should be glad if I could flatter myself that I came as near to the central idea of the occasion, in two hours, as you did in two minutes." So too, I would like to flatter myself to think that all of my long winded sermons come as near to the heart of hope as Dr. Carver's one minute missives contained herein.

R. Courtney Krueger, M.Div. D. Min.
Senior Minister
First Cumberland Presbyterian Church
Chattanooga, Tennessee

Other CSS Publishing titles authored by Gary L. Carver.

Out From the Ordinary
Acting on the Absurd
Distinctly Different
Search for Serendipity
Living a Victorious Life (with Tom Garritson)

GOTTA MINUTE?

60 – SECOND STORIES THAT SPEAK OF LIFE AND FAITH

GARY L. CARVER

CSS Publishing Company, Inc.
Lima, Ohio

Gotta Minute?

FIRST EDITION

Library of Congress Cataloging-in-Publication Data: Pending

Names: Carver, Gary L., 1946- author.
Title: Gotta minute : sixty - second stories that speak of life / Gary l Carver.
Description: First edition. | Lima, Ohio : CSS Publishing Company, Inc., [2020] | Includes index. | Identifiers: LCCN 2020040814 | ISBN 9780788029608 | ISBN 0788029606 | ISBN 9780788029615 (ebook) | ISBN 0788029614 (ebook)
Subjects: LCSH: Story sermons. Classification: LCC BV4307.S7 C37 2020 | DDC 252--dc23 LC record available at https://lccn.loc.gov/2020040814

For more information about CSS Publishing Company resources, visit our website at www.csspub.com, email us at csr@csspub.com, or call (800) 241-4056.

e-book:
ISBN-13: 978-0-7880-2961-5
ISBN-10: 0-7880-2961-4

ISBN-13: 978-0-7880-2960-8
ISBN-10: 0-7880-2960-6

DIGITALLY PRINTED

FOR SHARLON

Contents

PREFACE

"Gotta Minute? ...Gary Carver here, with a word from..." For over 35 years those words have rung out over a dozen different radio and television stations and are often included in magazines and newspapers.

I have never been much of a pulpiteer, orator, or theologian. I guess that if the good Lord gave me a strength, it might be that I am a storyteller. I love stories. God has given to me the gift to see stories in the everyday lives of people, and the love of telling these stories, that people just like you may see spiritual truth. Hopefully, from my little stories, you will be able to incorporate these spiritual truths into your own story.

I am a country storyteller. I guess that is not too bad, for over sixty years ago, someone told me a story. It was the greatest story ever told. Since I heard that story, I have never been the same. Now, God has given to me the glorious privilege of making it the business of my life to tell that wonderful story as I see it re-enacted in the lives of people just like you.

The collection of these little stories is the result of the efforts of a lifetime of the love for and the telling of stories. The reader will notice that, by design, there is no effort to name, label, or categorize these stories. The desire was to let each story stand on its own, to carry its message of truth. The "one minute message" is only one possible way to perceive the truth. The reader may inductively discover others as the Spirit leads. Thus, the side-door approach of allowing the story to carry the full weight of the truth.

My deepest gratitude goes to the First Baptist Church of Tuscumbia, Alabama, the First Baptist Church of Chattanooga, Tennessee, and the First Cumberland Presbyterian Church of Chattanooga, Tennessee, for the thousands of dollars, over decades, spent to sponsor *Gotta Minute?*

I also want to thank my loyal secretaries, Judy Lamon, Marguerite Copeland, Nan Griffith, Jo Ann Renegar, Judy Sullivan, Tammi Long, and Janice Guider for their tireless efforts to record, categorize, type and preserve my little stories.

A huge debt of gratitude goes to Pam Carver, our daughter-in-law, who edited and typed this manuscript. Her efforts made this a better book.

A special tip of the hat goes to a Chattanooga legend, Johnny Eagle. He knows why. Along with Johnny, I wish to thank Rabbi Ken Kanter, Rear Admiral Vance Fry, and Dr. Courtney Krueger for their generous endorsements.

Last, but never least, I want to thank my wife, confidant, and best friend for over fifty years, Sharlon. "Still pretty as a picture, and generous to a fault." One of the most striking comments about prayer was once stated by the comedian, Mel Brooks. He said "I don't pray. God gave to me Ann Bancroft. I have no right to ask for anything else." And God gave to me, Sharlon.

Khrushchev

Matthew 4:1-11

Ian MacPherson tells the following story: As he came under the influence of Christian teaching in 1903, this young boy showed an increasing interest in and enthusiasm for the Bible. He sought out the friendship of the local priest. He attended the confirmation classes and became familiar with the catechism. He went to the priest's house every Sunday to learn how to be a good Christian.

Once, he was awarded a prize for learning the four gospels by heart and reciting them word for word in church. From such an unbelievable beginning, this young man went on to become one of the most, if not *the* most powerful men in the world and the leader of his nation.

Who was this young man who, in at least some eyes, fulfilled the vast potential that was within him? His name was Nikita Khrushchev, the Soviet premier of Communist Russia.

ONE MINUTE MESSAGE: It is important to know not only the words of scripture, but the spirit of love contained therein.

Ben Hooper

Romans 8:12-16

He started life with one strike against him because his mother was not married. Living in a small community many years ago, he was the subject of jokes and questions. "Wonder who Ben's daddy is?" "Who's your father, boy?" Because of the jokes and taunts, he kept to himself.

When he was twelve years old, a new preacher came to town. Ben went to the church services to hear him. Before he could leave, the preacher came up to him, put his hand on Ben's head and said, "Now whose boy are you?"

Immediately the lad began to think, "Oh no! Here it comes again!"

Before he could respond, the preacher said, "I know who you are. I can see the family resemblance. I know who your daddy is. You are a child of God. You've got quite an inheritance there, young man. Go out and claim it." And he hid.

And we elected him governor of Tennessee, twice. His name was Hooper.

ONE MINUTE MESSAGE: Your inheritance as a child of God is yours to claim.

Higgins

2 Corinthians 4:13-18

Margaret Higgins was a war correspondent who received the Pulitzer Prize for her coverage of the Korean Conflict; specifically her account of the Fifth Marines. The Fifth Marines had originally numbered 18,000 when they met 100,000 Chinese communists in battle. That particular day was bitterly cold, 42 degrees below zero.

The weary, half-frozen soldiers stood around their dirty trucks, eating from tin cans. A huge Marine was eating cold beans with his trench knife. His clothes were stiff as a board. His face, covered with a heavy beard, was crusted with mud. Higgins asked him, "If I were God and could grant anything you wished, what would you wish for?"

The man stood motionless for a moment, and then he raised his head and replied, "Give me tomorrow."

ONE MINUTE MESSAGE: With God, there is always tomorrow.

Eisenhower

Romans 8:15-17

In January of 1953, Dwight David Eisenhower was being inaugurated as the 34th President of the United States. Everyone was interested in the war hero who was now elected president. Eisenhower's wife, brother and mother were being hounded by the press for any hint of insight about the nation's new leader.

President Eisenhower's mother was being interviewed by a particular reporter and asked questioningly, "This has to be a wonderful day for you. I know you are very proud of your son?" Her reply was, "Which one?"

ONE MINUTE MESSAGE: All of God's children are equal in his sight.

Special Olympics

Hebrews 10:19-24

Bob French told the story of a few years ago at the Seattle Special Olympics, when nine contestants, all physically or mentally disabled, assembled at the starting line for the 100-yard dash. At the gun, they all started out, not exactly in a dash, but with the relish to run the race to the finish and win.

All, that is, except one boy who stumbled on the asphalt, tumbled over a couple of times, and began to cry. The other eight heard the boy cry. They slowed down and paused. Then they all turned around and went back. Every one of them. One girl with Down's Syndrome bent down, kissed him, and said, "This will make it better." Then all nine linked arms and walked together to the finish line.

Everyone in the stadium stood, and the cheering went on for ten minutes.

ONE MINUTE MESSAGE: The real winners are those who love.

Wheel Barrow

James 2:18-26

Once there was a man who had the dream of crossing Niagara Falls on a tightrope. After considerable practice and the consistent encouragement of his neighbor, the man was able to accomplish this seemingly impossible feat.

Elated with the conquering of this challenge, he wanted to go even further. He now not only wanted to cross the falls on a tightrope again, but to do so pushing a man in a wheelbarrow.

The fateful day came, but the tightrope walker was hesitant. Again the neighbor was encouraging, "You must go on," he said. "You have done it once. I know you can do it again." To which the man asked, "Do you really believe I can? Do you really believe I can push a wheelbarrow across Niagara Falls with a man inside it?"

The neighbor responded, "Of course, I do!" The man replied, "Great! Get in the wheelbarrow!"

ONE MINUTE MESSAGE: Faith is an action word.

Free Lunch

Luke 9:57-62

The tale is told of an ancient king who gathered the learned men of his kingdom together. "Please sirs," he said, "gather together the wisdom of the ages in a form that can be taught to my people."

With that imperative as their mandate, the learned men spent ten years to accomplish their task. They proudly returned from their research with ten thick, beautifully bound volumes, appropriately title, *The Wisdom Of The Ages*.

The king responded, "Impressive, but it is too much. How can this ever be taught to my people? Return to your task… condense, refine," it is good, but too much. Return to your task and condense for me the wisdom of the ages in a form that can be taught to my people."

The scholars returned in only one day. "Sir, our deliberation is complete. We have refined the wisdom of the ages not to ten volumes, not to one thick volume, but to five words. The wisdom of the ages, oh dear king, is simply this: There ain't no free lunch."

ONE MINUTE MESSAGE: God's love is free, but in response, it will cost you everything you have.

Namath

Psalms 103:1-12

They said that Willie might become All-American, but he would never become a man. Willie was a good athlete, but he was not very mature. He had the reputation for being very fond of staying out all night, drinking a lot, and breaking training rules. Right before the biggest football game of his life, he broke training rules again.

His grouchy old coach said, "Willie, you are the best athlete I have ever coached, but you are not a man and you cannot play football for me anymore."

In spite of his potential, Willie was thrown off the team. His career was finished.

Years later, when Willie was inducted into the Pro Football Hall of Fame, he first of all thanked God. He then went on to thank his grouchy old coach, now deceased, for giving him a second chance. That was the day that Willie… Joe Willie… Joe Willie Namath became a man.

ONE MINUTE MESSAGE: With God there is always a second chance, and a third, a fourth…

Stalin

1 Kings 18:16-21

In 1893, a young man entered the Tifalis Theological Seminary to fulfill his sense of God's calling to become a priest. For five years he studied diligently to prepare himself for that task, but was then expelled from the school for reading a book that was considered unfit for young theological minds.

When that door slammed in his face, he turned his attention and gifts toward the political arena. Eventually he became a very powerful man, and more than any other single person, he was responsible for the imprisonment and death of at least twenty million people.

His name was Josef Stalin.

ONE MINUTE MESSAGE: Service in God's kingdom is closed to none and open to all.

Carl Joseph

2 Corinthians 4:7-12

Zig Ziglar told the story of Carl Joseph, a star all-around athlete with Madison High School Cougars in Madison, Florida. He could dunk a basketball. He high-jumped five feet, ten inches. In all, he won thirteen varsity letters in high school, but where he most excelled was in football, where he played on the defensive line.

He was especially good in sacking the quarterback. In the homecoming game of his junior year, he made twelve tackles and led his team to a 6 — 0 victory.

What was so unusual about Carl Joseph? Nothing, except this young man avoided the road of self-pity and won thirteen varsity letters in spite of the fact that he only had one leg.

ONE MINUTE MESSAGE: Courage and determination can overcome almost any obstacle.

Boy And Old Man

Psalms 24:1-10

A young boy and an old man sat on the dock in the late afternoon, fishing. They had talked about many things. They had talked about why sunsets are red, why the rain falls, why the seasons change, and why the grass is green.

Finally the little boy looked up at the old man and asked. "Grandpa, does anyone ever see God?" the old man stopped baiting the hook for the young lad and looked wistfully across the blue waters. "Son," he said, "it is getting so I hardly see anything else."

ONE MINUTE MESSAGE: Seek to see the hand of God in all of his creation.

Alex Haley

1 Chronicles 28:19-21

For as long as he could remember, Alex wanted to be a writer. For eight years he wrote stories and articles for publication, and for eight long years he received nothing but rejection slips.

But he did not give up, even though for eight years he was never able to publish a single story.

Then one day an editor sent him another rejection slip, but on the bottom he wrote two words: "Nice try."

By this simple note of encouragement, the young writer was moved to tears and was given new hope. He kept on writing until, after many years of effort, he a wrote book that deeply affected the entire world. That was when Alex, Alex Haley, wrote the award winning book, *Roots*.

ONE MINUTE MESSAGE: Through hard work, hope, and encouragement, dreams can come true.

Fall Down, Get Up

1 John 1:5-10

John Claypool beautifully illustrated the nature of the Christian life with the following story. Years ago, a monastery stood on the side of a mountain and a village lay below. One day, one of the monks came to the village for supplies. One of the villagers ran up to him with great enthusiasm. "Holy Father," he said, "surely yours is the greatest of lives. Tell me, please, what do you do all day long up there in the monastery, so high in the mountains, so close to God?"

The monk thought a minute and answered simply, "Well, my son, it is like this: we fall down and we get up. We fall down and we get up. We fall down and we get up."

ONE MINUTE MESSAGE: God's power is the power to get up again.

Mrs. Gadabout

Philippians 4:10-13

Phillip Keller, the shepherd, told the story of the ewe that once belonged to him. In every way, she was outstanding. Her body was beautiful, her constitution was strong, she had an excellent coat of wool, and she bore sturdy lambs that matured rapidly.

In spite of all these attractive attributes, she had one pronounced fault: she was restless, discontented, and a fence crawler to the extent that Keller nicknamed her "Mrs. Gadabout."

She spent her entire life looking for greener pastures so much so that she not only led her own lambs to do this, but other sheep as well. She was never contented with things as they were.

Because she was such a bad influence, Keller eventually had to get rid of her.

ONE MINUTE MESSAGE: True contentment comes as a result of trust in the resources of God.

Crete

Revelation 22:12-13

An elderly man lay dying on his beloved island of Crete. So in love with the land was he that as he died, he asked to be laid on the land. As he passed, he grasped two handfuls of his beloved soil.

He awoke to find himself before the pearly gates. They said, "You are welcome, but you cannot bring the soil in here." "Then I will not come in," he said.

After numerous attempts to urge him beyond the gates, one of his granddaughters came to him. "Grandpa, we miss you. Please come in, but you will have to leave the soil behind."

Unable to resist her pleading, he dropped the soil and entered heaven. The first thing he saw was his beloved island.

ONE MINUTE MESSAGE: If we are to take hold of God's hand, we must turn loose of everything else.

Santa Claus, Indiana

Psalms 95:1-7

Several years ago, when we were still in graduate school and our three sons were small, we made a trip to Santa Claus, Indiana.

As one can imagine, the entire city is built around the Christmas theme. There we found a post office, where many of the letters that are written to Santa are received. It was interesting to talk to the postmaster. He told me that in the previous year, thousands upon thousands of letters had been sent to Santa Claus, expressing desires for Christmas gifts. Can you guess how many letters were received expressing gratitude for the gifts after Christmas? One! Only one!

ONE MINUTE MESSAGE: Christmas should be a time for giving gifts and gratitude.

Bobby Richardson

Acts 1:7-8

LeVan Parker told the story of Bobby Richardson, a dedicated Christian who once played second base for the New York Yankees. The Yankees were playing the Giants in the World Series. The brothers, Mattie and Felipe Alou, were teammates on the Giants.

Felipe, also a dedicated Christian, spoke to Bobby before the game. "If you get an opportunity," he said, "I would appreciate your speaking a word to Mattie, for he is not a Christian."

The game began. In one of the middle innings during a very tight ballgame, Mattie came to the plate. He stroked a hard single to left field. The left fielder bobbled the ball, and Felipe Alou took off for second base.

Richardson, covering second base, took the throw from the left fielder, swept the ball down, tagging Alou "out." Before thousands in Yankee Stadium and millions in the television audience, he said, "Mattie, why don't you give your heart and life to Jesus?"

ONE MINUTE MESSAGE: Always is a good time to give witness to the life with us.

Mill And Carlyle

1 Kings 7:1-10

When the English historian Thomas Carlyle finished his manuscript on the French Revolution, he gave it to his friend, John Stuart Mill, to review.

Several days later, Mill came to Carlyle's home and regretfully revealed that his maid had used the manuscript to start a fire. Carlyle was in a frenzy! Two years of labor was lost! He was in such a state of depression that he could not write again. Then one day he saw a mason, building a large wall one brick at a time. With this inspiration, he decided to begin again by writing one page at a time.

Guess what happened? His second manuscript was better than the first.

ONE MINUTE MESSAGE: Live each day to its fullest.

Bill Russell

1 Thessalonians 5:16-24

Few would dispute the fact that Bill Russell of Boston was the greatest basketball player of all time, leading his Celtics to eleven world championships in thirteen seasons; a record that will never be broken.

Once, in the final game of the NBA Championship Series, Russell stepped to the line for a pair of free throws in a very close game. If he made the shots, the Celtics would again be on their way to another title.

As he was about to shoot, one of his teammates came over and said something to the giant center. Russell grinned and then sank two free throws. Again, the Celtics were champions of the world!

After the game, a reporter asked Larry Siegfried, the Celtic guard, what he said to Russell? "Well, sometimes 'Russ' forgets to bend his knees. I just reminded him to do that."

ONE MINUTE MESSAGE: If the greatest basketball player who ever lived had to be reminded of the basics of his game, how much more do we need to let God remind us of the basics of the game of life?

ChapStick®

Psalms 139:23-24

Several weeks ago I was standing in the line in the hardware store waiting to pay for my purchases when I noticed a woman drive up, get out of her pickup, and walk in the front door.

She came to the register and placed a 99-cents tube of ChapStick® on the counter. "I did not buy this," she said. "It must have fallen in my sack." She then left with no further word.

I remarked to the sales clerk, "Now there is an honest woman." She replied, "Yes, and they are so rare these days."

I thought to myself on the way home, "Why did she go to all that trouble to return a 99-cents tube of ChapStick®? Why didn't she keep it? Who would have known?"

Then I thought, "She would have known. That is who."

ONE MINUTE MESSAGE: Play your life to an audience of one who sees and knows all.

Oil Refinery

Romans 14:5-8

Anthony Campolo told about a man who was going on a tour of an oil refinery. The tour guide showed him the various aspects of the refining process and the various departments in which those presses are carried out. At the end of the tour, the man asked the guide the simple question, "Where is the shipping department?"

"Shipping department? What shipping department?"

The man continued, "I am looking for the place where all the gasoline and oil products in this plant are shipped out for use in the world at large."

"Oh," said the tour guide. "You don't understand. All the energy generated in this refinery is used to keep the refinery going."

ONE MINUTE MESSAGE: The fullness of life is experienced when we go beyond ourselves.

Les Miserables

John 3:16-18

Victor Hugo's masterpiece, *Les Miserables*, was a study in contrasts of two men who have been touched by grace and forgiveness

Jean Valjean, the main character, was forgiven by a priest for stealing two silver candlesticks. This touch of grace and forgiveness changed his life. He was converted, and the remainder of his life was a reflection of the grace and forgiveness he experienced from the priest.

The other individual was Javert, the police officer who continued to pursue Valjean over the theft. When Javert was caught in a life or death situation, Valjean freed him, forgave him, and granted him life.

Javert, a man of unbending rules and stern prejudice, could not cope with forgiveness. The man who had every reason to hate him instead forgave him and then gave to Javert his life. Because he could not accept that forgiveness, Javert committed suicide by throwing himself into the River Seine.

ONE MINUTE MESSAGE: Each of us, when touched by God's grace, will either become a reflection of that grace or will choose the road of self-destruction when we fail to forgive others.

Johnny And All A's

Luke 15:11-20

Johnny bounced off the bus with excitement. It was report card day, and Johnny had all "A's." Well — one A-minus.

He ran into the kitchen where his mother stood. "It's report card day, huh? Let me see! That's good, Johnny, but of course, you always do well. I had forgotten it was report card day. I hope your sister pulled up her low grade in special education."

Johnny ran in the den where his father sat. "What have you got, Slugger? Report card, huh? Straight A's again! That's neat. Hey, what's that A-minus doing there? Oh, well — wonder who is playing Monday night football?"

As Johnny took his card from his father and walked to his room, he thought, "Surely straight A's deserves at least one hug."

ONE MINUTE MESSAGE: Experience the acceptance of God.

Houdini

Revelation 3:20-22

The great magician Harry Houdini was the greatest escape artist in the history of the world. He unlocked every door that was ever put before him except one. He was taken to a castle in the British Isles, placed inside a room, and was given the task to unlock the door. He worked on it for over two hours. He tried every trick he knew, but he could not unlock the door. After two hours and total exhaustion, he collapsed, fell against the door, and the door opened. The door had never been locked.

ONE MINUTE MESSAGE: The door to God's grace is always open.

Brought Father Lunch

1 Corinthians 12:1-27

Sandy Wylie told the story of a little girl who was sitting on the steps of a large cathedral that was newly built. A man who was passing by paused for a moment to admire the beautiful architecture. He was surprised to hear the little girl speak up: "Do you like it?"

"Yes, I think it is very beautiful," the man answered.

"I'm glad you like it," replied the little girl, "because I helped build it."

The man smiled and said, "You are awfully small to have had a part in the construction of such a large building. Tell me, what did you do?"

The little girl proudly announced, "My father is a bricklayer. He worked on this church; and every day he worked, I brought his lunch."

ONE MINUTE MESSAGE: In God's vineyard, we all have a part to play.

Both Thieves

Romans 3:21-26

The worship service was over, and the offering plate filled with money was lying on the communion table. A five-year-old boy by the name of Peter took $5 out of the plate. Quietly the pastor placed his hand on the boy's shoulder and, "Peter, don't you think you want to put that money back?"

"Please, please, don't tell my daddy," he said. "He'll kill me."

Knowing that the punishment would not be quite that severe, the pastor did tell the father. The father immediately responded, "I'm going to kill that kid!" The pastor said, "Before you act in haste, you might remember that possibly there was a time in your life when you stole something also."

He reminded the father of how he, too, had stolen a dozen eggs. The father relayed this story to his son and in a mutual moment of love, they hugged each other. Peter exclaimed. "Oh, Daddy, I'm so happy! We're both thieves!"

ONE MINUTE MESSAGE: All of us are in the same lot.

Henry Seigler

1 John 1:1-10

The story of Henry Seigler was told in the August 30, 1982 edition of "Newsweek." Henry Seigler was accused of robbery and the murder of a Richmond, Virginia insurance agent. He was put on trial for his life. He pleaded not guilty, but as the jury deliberated his fate, he became very nervous and decided to accept a plea bargain. As his lawyers were informing the judge, the jury stood outside the courtroom with the verdict. If Henry Seigler had waited three more minutes, he would have heard the verdict — *not guilty*. Despite the verdict, Seigler was given a sixty-year prison sentence.

ONE MINUTE MESSAGE: When we know we are right, it is best to keep on keeping on.

Irving McPringle

Philippians 3:12-14

A father wanted to encourage his young son who was upset about his schoolwork. "Just don't give up!" the father encouraged.

"Remember, Robert Fulton didn't give up. Albert Einstein didn't give up. Florence Nightingale didn't give up. Thomas Edison didn't give up. And then there was Irving McPringle."

"Who was Irving McPringle?" was the question from the little boy. To which his father replied, "See, you never heard of him. He gave up!"

ONE MINUTE MESSAGE: The door to the future is often opened by the hand of adversity.

Feed Everybody?

Ephesians 4:1-6

Amid the ruin and rubble of war-torn Germany, a group of Quakers were feeding people in the hollowed-out shell of a half-burned building. A desperate and half-starved Polish woman stumbled up to the efforts to minister among the humiliation and horrors of war.

She asked the Quakers, "Do you feed everybody?" "Yes," was the reply.

"Poles?"

"Yes."

"Germans?"

"Yes."

"Russians?"

"Yes."

"Jews?"

"Yes."

"Atheists?"

"Yes."

The woman drew a deep sigh and said, "I knew there ought to be people like that in the world, but I did not know where they were."

ONE MINUTE MESSAGE: Share the bread of life with any and all who will come.

Master's Voice

John 10:14-15

During World War II, a group of tired and weary soldiers were huddled on the battlefield during a lull in combat around a worn out phonograph. Playing on the phonograph was an old, beaten up, scratched record. The record was a recording of Enrico Caruso, the "Master's Voice," at that time considered to be the greatest voice in the world.

Amid the horror and death of war, there was a voice of poetry. Amid the pain, suffering and evil, there was music. And they listened.

Some listened and complained because it was so much trouble to set up the phonograph. Others complained because the record was beaten up, scratched, and contained a lot of static. And there were a select few who listened for the master's voice.

ONE MINUTE MESSAGE: Amid the pain and suffering of life, we can always choose to listen to the master's voice.

Sandburg Exclusive

Romans 10:14-15

Fred Craddock told the story of Carl Sandburg, that master of the use of words who was being interviewed on television. The commentator asked, "What is the ugliest word in the human language?" As the air filled with an expectant silence, Sandburg sat and questioned, "The ugliest word in the human language…" He bowed his head as though he was looking for a word on the floor. Then he looked up at the ceiling, as though he would pull one out of the air.

He mumbled again, "The ugliest word…" Television viewers gathered on the edge of their chairs. "Ugliest," he said, still searching for the word.

Then as expectation was at its highest, he rubbed his chin and said, "To me, the ugliest word in the human language is 'exclusive.'"

ONE MINUTE MESSAGE: With God, no one is excluded.

Little Sachi

Acts 3:17-20

Dan Willman related the story of little Sachi. Soon after her brother was born, little Sachi began to ask her parents to leave her alone with the new baby. They worried that, like most four-year-olds, she might feel jealous and want to hit or shake him, so they refused. But she showed no signs of jealousy. She treated the baby with kindness and her pleas to be left alone with him became more urgent. They decided to allow it.

Elated, she went into the baby's room and shut the door, but it opened a crack — enough for her curious parents to peek in and listen. They saw little Sachi walk quietly up to her baby brother, put her face close to his and say quietly, "Baby, tell me what God feels like. I'm starting to forget."

ONE MINUTE MESSAGE: Returning to God is an act of the will.

Hound And Stagg

Matthew 22:34-40

Have you heard the fable of the bloodhound that started in a hunt chasing a magnificent stag? As he was chasing it, a fox crossed the path, so the hound chased the fox. After a while, a rabbit crossed the path, so the hound chased the rabbit.

Later on a mouse crossed the path, and the hound chased the mouse until it ran into a mouse hole.

The hound began his hunt on the trail of a magnificent stag, and he ended up staring into a mouse hole.

ONE MINUTE MESSAGE: It often is difficult to keep our priorities in life.

People Downtown

1 Timothy 5:3-8

Keith Miller told of his early experience of trying to develop a more meaningful prayer life. One particular morning, he got up very early and stumbled around the house until he had caused everyone in the house to be awake.

Two of his daughters, ages seven and five, began to tiptoe quietly in and ask, "What are you doing, Daddy, and why are you reading that book?" Frustrated by the intrusion, he became very irritated. He screamed at the children to, "Be quiet and get out of here… Daddy's busy!" The youngest daughter, sniffling back tears, asked her mother through the kitchen door, "What is the matter with Daddy?"

His wife calmly replied, "Oh, he is learning how to be a good Christian so that he can love the people downtown."

ONE MINUTE MESSAGE: If we are not a Christian at home, where are we?

Johnny Majors

Proverbs 12:17-22

I liked Johnny when he was an outstanding high school football player and a member of Tennessee's most favorite football family. I liked Johnny when he was an undersized, All-American running back for the Volunteer single wing and I still feel like he should have won the Heisman.

I liked Johnny when he took a dilapidated program at Iowa State, turned it around and then guided Tony Dorsett and the Pittsburgh Panthers to the national championship.

I liked Johnny when he heard his mama call and returned home to guide the fortunes of the Big Orange. But I think I liked Johnny best when he had the courage to suspend his running back for disciplinary reasons. That was when Johnny "majored" on something important — that character, class, and integrity are more important than winning football games.

ONE MINUTE MESSAGE: Honesty is always the best policy.

"Weigh Kids?"

Philippians 3:7-11

Fred Craddock told the story of Glen Adsett, a missionary in China. He was under house arrest in China when the soldiers came one day and said, "You can return to America." They were celebrating, and the soldiers said, "You can take two hundred pounds with you." They had been there for years — two hundred pounds.... They got the scales and started the family argument — two children, wife, husband. We must have this vase. This is a new typewriter. What about my books? What about this? They weighed everything and took it off. They weighed this and took it off then weighed this and, finally, right on the dot — two hundred pounds. The soldiers asked, "Ready to go?" "Yes." "Did you weigh everything?" "Yes." "You weighed the kids?" "Weigh the kids." And in a moment, typewriter, vase, and all became trash.

ONE MINUTE MESSAGE: Adversity often provides the opportunity to re-access what is important.

Boy And Sunday School

Hebrews 10:19-25

The young lad turned over slowly in the bed as his father yelled throughout the house. “Get up! It’s time to go to Sunday school. Up and at ‘em. Time to get ready.”

The boy mumbled, “Oh Dad, do we have to?”

“You bet!”, the father replied. “Get up! It’s important that you go to church.”

“If it is so important, why don’t you come with us?” the boy asked.

“Sure it is important. Get up and get ready to go.”

“Tell me Dad, did you go to Sunday school when you were a boy?”

“Sure, son, I went then.”

The young boy arose from his bed, mumbling under his breath. “It probably won’t do me any good either.”

ONE MINUTE MESSAGE: Good habits, started young, can influence a lifetime.

Nancy And Todd Lincoln

Proverbs 27:1

Back in Kentucky, the old-timers used to tell of that cold day in February of 1809 when a rural mail carrier made his weekly trip through Hardin County. A local citizen met him at a crossroad and inquired about what was going on in the outside world. The mail carrier reported there was talk of a National Bank and it looked like there might be trouble brewing again between the United States and Great Britain. Then the mail carrier turned the conversation around and said, "Tell me, what is happening in these parts?"

To which the local man answered, "Shucks, mister, nothin' ever happens back here. There was a baby born last night to Nancy Hanks and Tom Lincoln, but shucks, mister, nothin' ever happens back here."

ONE MINUTE MESSAGE: Who knows what a day may bring?

Fiddler On The Roof

John 21:15-19

Do you remember Tevye and Golde in *Fiddler on the Roof*? They were a married couple who lived in a Russian village where everyone knew everyone else. Tevye, a dairyman, was marrying off his five daughters, one by one. Try as he may, he could not persuade them to marry the men he had chosen for them. Each girl in turn fell in love, and the man she loved was the only husband she would have. After giving approval, reluctantly, to the second daughter, who was deliriously in love, Tevye began to think about his own marriage. He turned to Golde, and he asked, "Do you love me?"

"Do I what?"

"Do you love me?"

"What kind of question is that?" asked Golde. "Go lie down. You must have indigestion."

"Golde, I'm asking you a question — do you love me?"

"Do I love you? For 25 years I've washed your clothes, cooked your meals, cleaned your house, given you children, milked the cow. After 25 years, why talk about love right now?"

"Golde, the first time I met you was our wedding day. I was scared, I wondered if we would get on together. But my father and mother said we'd learn to love each other. And now I'm asking, Golde, do you love me?"

"Do I love him? For 25 years I've lived with him, fought with him, shared with him for 25 years my bed. If that's not love, what is?"

"Then you love me?"

“I suppose I do.”

“And I suppose I love you, too.”

Tevye and Golde then sing together, and their song says basically that it doesn’t change a thing, but after 25 years, it’s nice to know.

ONE MINUTE MESSAGE: Is there anyone you need to speak to?

Edgar Bergen

Genesis 12:1-4

When Edgar sent off to the mail order house and ordered a book on photography, he waited for the mailman to come every day. Finally the mailman did come with a package. When Edgar opened the package, he was terribly disappointed — even angry — because they had not sent him the book on photography he had ordered. They had sent him a book on ventriloquism.

He immediately began to return the book but on second thought, decided that he might as well determine what he could with it. In fact, he did quite well because Edgar was soon accompanied by Charlie — Charlie McCarthy and Mortimer Snerd.

Edgar's last name, of course, is Bergen.

ONE MINUTE MESSAGE: When we are disappointed with the lemons of life, we can make lemonade.

Charge Of Chicken

2 Corinthians 8:1-5

The governor of Massachusetts was running hard for a second term. He had campaigned all morning, missed lunch, and arrived late in the afternoon at a large barbecue.

As he held out his plate, the tired woman serving the plate put one piece of chicken on it. “Excuse me,” he said, “May I have another piece of chicken?” “Sorry, only one piece to a customer,” she replied.

“I beg your pardon,” he continued. “Don’t you know me? I am Christian Herter, I am the governor of this state!” “And I am the lady in charge of the chicken.” she said, “one piece to a customer. Now move along, Mister!”

ONE MINUTE MESSAGE: Who is in charge of your life?

Can I Ask The Blessing?

Matthew 5:1-12

My good friend, Dr. Tommy Garrison, told me a story this past week of when he served a church in another city. After the Sunday morning service, a couple came up to him with faces downcast. They said, "Pastor, we've got to make some changes in our lives." He said, "Well, I noticed that you've not been in church for a while."

"We've got to make some changes in our lives. Last evening, we had a party at our home. There were many people there and it was quite loud. Some people were probably doing things they should not have been doing. It got out of hand and caused our four year old daughter to wake up. She came down the stairs and saw all of the people and the food and all the glasses sitting around. She said, 'Oh boy, we're about to eat! Can I ask the blessing?'"

ONE MINUTE MESSAGE: What are we asking God to bless?

Hope To Lose

Romans 8:28-29

Nikos Kazantzakis told of an earnest young man who went to a remote island, where hermits had been living for generations in their solitary search for God. In talking to a saintly old hermit one day, he asked, “Tell me, father, do you still wrestle with the devil?”

To which the old man answered, “Oh no, my son, I have grown too old for that. Now I wrestle with God.”

“With God?” the young man exclaimed in astonishment, “but do you hope to win?”

“Oh no, my child,” he answered quietly, “I hope to lose.”

ONE MINUTE MESSAGE: Our greatest battle is between what we are and what he is.

Lucky Dog

1 John 4:7-12

Buckner Fanning told of several years ago, in the "Lost and Found" section of a midwestern newspaper, there appeared the following article:

LOST DOG: Brown fur, some missing due to mange. Blind in one eye, partially deaf. Limps because of recent automobile accident. Slightly arthritic. Answers to the name of "LUCKY".

The first time I heard that, I laughed as possibly you did. I could picture in my mind this old brown, skinny, mangy dog, limping around, arthritic, crippled, half-deaf, half-blind, half-dead, and answers to the name of "Lucky"?

But, you know, he *was* lucky. He was a lucky dog. Why? Someone wanted him. Someone spent money to retrieve him. He was a lucky dog because he was loved.

ONE MINUTE MESSAGE: We are lucky dogs because God loves us.

Send For Foreman

Isaiah 58:9-11

The story is told of a textile factory where this sign was on the wall over each machine:

"If your threads get tangled, send for the foreman."

A new employee went to work, and soon the threads became badly tangled. The more she sought to untangle them, the more helpless she became. Finally, after wasting a lot of time, she did call for the foreman.

When the foreman came, he asked, "Why didn't you send for me earlier?" The employee replied in her defense, "I did my best!" To which the foreman answered, "Remember, doing your best *is* sending for me!"

ONE MINUTE MESSAGE: Often, the best thing we can do is to let go and let God.

Bart Starr

Romans 12:3-8

Bart Starr, the great Super Bowl winning quarterback of the Green Bay Packers, made an arrangement one year with his oldest son, Bart Jr., to encourage good grades. For every "A" that Bart Jr. brought home from school, Dad would give him ten cents (You have to remember this was the 1960's).

One Sunday, the Packers had a particularly bad game, and Starr did not play well at all. It was a long plane ride home, but as he arrived and entered his own bedroom, he felt encouraged to see a handwritten note from Bart Jr. It read:

Dear Dad, I thought you played a great game.
Love,
Bart

Taped to the note were two dimes.

ONE MINUTE MESSAGE: Left any dimes around lately?

Mother's Translation

2 Timothy 1:3-8

Four ministers were talking one day about translations of the Bible. One said, "I like the King James Version best. The beauty of the language and the rhythm of the cadence is unsurpassed."

Another said, "I like the Revised Standard Version because it is the closest to the actual Greek and Hebrew tongues."

Another said, "I like the New International Version because it is so easy to read."

The fourth thought a moment and then he said, "Of all the translations, I think I like my mother's the best."

One said, "You mean your mother has translated the Bible?"

He said, "Oh yes, every day she translated the Bible to me in her life of love, compassion, forgiveness, and sacrifice. Because of her translation, I trusted Jesus Christ as my Savior."

ONE MINUTE MESSAGE: Our lives may be the only Bible someone will ever read.

Louis Evan's Dog

Galatians 6:1-2

Louis Evans told of a dog that was run over by a car. A doctor hurriedly bound up its broken leg and took the dog into his own home. After weeks of care, he was surprised to discover that the dog had just walked off and left him. He had some harsh thoughts about that ungrateful dog.

Two days later, he heard a scratching at his front door and on the front porch he found the dog he had healed — in the company of another dog that had been hurt.

ONE MINUTE MESSAGE: Evangelism can be defined as one beggar telling another beggar where to find food.

Corrie And Betsy

1 Thessalonians 5:16-18

Corrie Ten Boom and her sister, Betsy, were victims of the Holocaust. They hid and protected individuals who otherwise might have been killed. When they were in a Nazi prison camp, it was such a flea-ridden, terrible place that they couldn't stand it. Betsy said, "But I have found something in the Bible that will help us. It says, 'In all things, give thanks.'"

Corrie said, "I can't give thanks for the fleas."

Betsy said, "Give thanks that we're together. Most families have been split up."

Corrie said, "I can do that."

Her sister continued, "Give thanks that somehow the guards didn't check our belongings and our Bible is with us." She gave thanks for that. But Corrie would not even think of giving thanks for the fleas.

Later, they found that the only reason they were not molested and harmed by the guards was because their captors were so repulsed by the fleas.

ONE MINUTE MESSAGE: Paul, the apostle, says "Give thanks in everything!"

Sins Run Behind Me

Romans 8:21-26

The Desert Fathers told the story of when one of the men in a certain community committed a serious sin. The council called a meeting and requested the minister to attend. When he refused to come, they sent a delegation telling him the matter was most urgent. "Since you insist," he said, "I will come in about thirty minutes."

When he arrived at the meeting of the council, the minister entered the room carrying a leaking jug on his back, filled with water. The members of the council asked, "Minister, what is this?"

"All day long," the minister replied, "my sins run out behind me and I am unaware of them. Yet despite my blindness to my own sin, today I am asked to judge the error of another."

When they heard the words of the man of God, they forgave the man who had sinned and said no more.

ONE MINUTE MESSAGE: We all are sinners saved by the grace of God.

Willard Scott

2 Peter 1:5-9

Willard Scott told the following story: It happened a few years ago as he was riding in a taxi in Washington, DC.

The taxi driver said, "I remember you when you were Ronald McDonald." Scott replied, "Oh, that's terrific!"

"Yes, I brought my little boy to see you. It was twenty years ago." The taxi driver continued, "Do you know what I remember most?" "What is that?" Willard asked.

"I was a Black Panther at the time, a member of a militant group. I hated white people. In all the crowds of kids who came up to you, when my little boy came up to you, his shoe was untied. I remember that you reached down and tied his shoe."

ONE MINUTE MESSAGE: The simple and kind acts of love bring us together as the brothers and sisters we are.

Karl Barth

John 3:16

Karl Barth has been called the greatest theologian of the early twentieth century. In his only visit to the United States, he was talking to a group of graduate students at Princeton University. A student asked, "Dr. Barth, in all of your years of study, what is the greatest truth you have ever discovered?"

A hush fell over the room. The students sat on the edge of their seats. The media sat poised with pen and paper to record his answer.

Barth thought a moment, pulled on his pipe, and in a serious tone, replied, "The greatest truth I have ever discovered in all my years of study is this:

Jesus loves me,
This I know.
For the Bible
Tells me so."

ONE MINUTE MESSAGE: The greatest truth can be the simplest — God loves us.

Tulip Blooming

2 Corinthians 1:3-7

Fred Craddock told this story: Their shovels were their fingernails, and their wheelbarrows were their skirts. Every day they went to work on cardboard shoes in the bitter, freezing cold. These were the Jewish women who survived the horrors of the WW II concentration camps. One such woman was asked, “How did you survive?”

“I don’t know,” she replied, “but I do remember one day as we marched to work, I saw a house that had a window flower box. In the box was a tulip blooming. I thought all day long, if I can endure today, maybe on the way home I’ll get to see the tulip again!”

A tulip blooming? Just a tulip?

ONE MINUTE MESSAGE: Hope can survive on a slender diet.

Stiffened Elbows

John 21:15-17

John Claypool told of the parable told of a man who dreamed he was transported to the next life and allowed to see the places called heaven and hell. It was explained that the one difference between people here and people on earth was that their elbows were stiffened.

The man was taken first to the lower region and there he saw a wretched scene of chaos and misery. The people had loaves of bread in their hands, but their elbows were stiffened, and they could not get the food to their mouths. It was total confusion and misery.

From there the man was taken to heaven, and the spirit of that place was totally different. Here there were harmony, creativity, and joy. Here, too, the people had food in their hands and stiffened elbows, but instead of being frustrated over their inability to feed themselves, they were lovingly feeding each other.

ONE MINUTE MESSAGE: The greatest joy is in giving to others.

One Follower

Matthew 6:24

S.I. McMillan told the story of a young woman who wanted to go to college, but her heart sank when she read the question on the application blank: Are you a leader?

Being both honest and conscientious, she wrote, "No," and returned the application, expecting the worst.

To her surprise, she received this letter from the college:

Dear Applicant,

A study of the application forms reveals that this year our college will have 1,452 new leaders. We are accepting you because we feel it is imperative that we have at least one follower.

ONE MINUTE MESSAGE: As said, "You're gonna have to serve somebody… might as well be the Lord."

E. V. Hill

Romans 8:31-32

John Sullivan told the story of E.V. Hill, a well-known African American preacher in Los Angeles. Hill told of a personal crisis he and his family faced during the Watts riots years ago. Another pastor had already been killed, and word was that Hill would be next. He received a threatening phone call. When his wife asked who had called, he said. "Some things you don't need to know." Sensing danger, she pressed Dr. Hill. Finally, he relented, saying, "The caller said, 'Don't be surprised if you discover a bomb in your car.'"

The next morning, he awoke to discover his car was gone. In a few minutes he saw the car pull around the corner and into the driveway. His wife got out of the car. Hill asked his wife, "Where have you been?"

She said, "I decided that if somebody was going to be killed, I'd rather it be me."

ONE MINUTE MESSAGE: How have we followed Jesus' example of others above ourselves?

Anson Mount

Mark 10:23-31

Fred Craddock told the story of Anson Mount, the religious editor of a national magazine. When he came to the time in his life to retire, he went back to his boyhood home just north of Nashville, Tennessee. He never gave it a second thought until he arrived at the small town. He looked around and asked himself, "What am I doing here? I have been away so long, no one knows me."

He pulled up to a country store that had a gas pump outside. After a moment or two, an old man shuffled down the steps, toothpick in his mouth, looked in the car window and waited. Mount said, "Uh, fill 'er up!"

The old man nodded his head and took his time going to the back of the car. It took seemingly forever for the old codger to pump the gas. Moving at his own pace, he put the hose up, closed the flap, and came around the car. The old man stuck his head in the window and asked, "Anson, do you want to pay for this now or put it on your bill?"

And Anson Mount was at home.

ONE MINUTE MESSAGE: God is the place where we find our true home.

Thinks I'm Real

James 1:19

Thomas Clifton told of when a waitress came to the table to take an order from a family. As she was going around the table, she looked at the young son and asked, "What will you have?" He didn't say a word. She said, "I bet you would like a hot dog."

The mother said, "He doesn't want a hot dog. He wants the special, all vegetables."

The waitress asked the young boy again, "Would you like a hot dog?" He nodded. The waitress asked, "Would you like catsup on that hot dog?"

The mother said, "No, he doesn't want a hot dog. He wants the special, all vegetables."

The waitress again looked at the little boy and asked, "Would you like a Coca-Cola with that hot dog?" He nodded, yes.

The mother was furious by this time, and said, "He will have the special, all vegetables." The waitress ignored her and walked back into the kitchen. The little boy looked up at his mother and said, "She thinks I'm real."

ONE MINUTE MESSAGE: Often, the best thing we can do is to listen.

Barney

Proverbs 3:5-6

Marilyn Thompson told the following story: A four-year-old girl was at the pediatrician's office for a check-up. As the doctor looked into her ears with an otoscope, he asked, "Do you think I'll find Big Bird in here?" The little girl stayed silent.

Next, the doctor took a tongue depressor and looked down her throat. He asked, "Do you think I'll find the Cookie Monster down there?" Again, the little girl was silent.

Then the doctor put a stethoscope to her chest. As he listened to her heartbeat, he asked, "Do you think I'll hear Barney in here?"

"Oh no!" the little girl replied. "Jesus is in my heart. Barney's on my underpants."

ONE MINUTE MESSAGE: Introduced anyone to Jesus? Barney, they probably already know.

Jimmy Carter Grass

Matthew 20:20-28

Todd Wilson said that for years, John Roberts had been the editor of *The Baptist Courier,* the state Baptist newspaper in South Carolina. One of his favorite stories was about a big car with an out of state license plate that stopped in front of the Maranatha Baptist Church in Plains, Georgia. A man in the car got out, camera in hand, to take a picture of the church where former President Jimmy Carter was a member. A fellow in overalls and a baseball cap was mowing the church lawn. He happened to be in the way of the picture the tourist wanted to take, so he asked the man mowing the lawn if he would move so he could take the picture. Without a word the workman smiled and pushed his mower out of the way.

A little later, the visitor was telling his story at one of the gift shops in Plains. The store owner asked if there had not been a fellow cutting the grass. The man explained that yes there had been, but he had been kind enough to move for him to take his picture.

"What a shame," the store owner exclaimed, "your picture would have been a real prize with the man and the lawnmower in it. You see, that was President Carter cutting the grass."

ONE MINUTE MESSAGE: The greatest of all is servant of all.

Bill Wymann

Matthew 7:24-27

Bill Wymann was a guitarist for the rock group, *The Rolling Stones*. According to Newsweek magazine, Bill Wymann married a woman who was 34 years younger than he was. His son, Stephen, married a woman who was sixteen years older than he was. Now where it gets confusing is that Stephen's wife is Bill's wife's mother. (The father married the daughter and the son married the mother) Stephen married his stepmother's mother. Bill married his daughter-in-law's daughter. Bill's wife married her mother's father-in-law and Stephen's wife married her daughter's stepson.

Now what will really get interesting is if Bill and his wife have a son. The boy's stepbrother will also be his grandfather, and in all of this, somebody is their own grandpa.

ONE MINUTE MESSAGE: To avoid confusion, build your family on the *rock*.

Billy Sunday

Romans 3:21-27

Billy Sunday, the great evangelist of another era, was preparing to preach a series of revival services in one of our nation's largest cities. He wrote to the mayor of that city and asked if he knew of individuals in that city who had spiritual problems or who were in the need of prayer, and to send him a list. Billy Sunday was indeed surprised when the big city mayor sent to him the entire city's telephone directory.

ONE MINUTE MESSAGE: It's me, Lord, standing in the need of prayer.

IBM Manager

Ephesians 2:1-10

Tim Hansel told the true story about a project manager at IBM who lost the company $10 million. Dejectedly, he walked into the president's office and said, "I am sorry. I am sure you will want my resignation. I will be gone by the end of the day."

The president's response showed his understanding of the value of failure. He said, "Are you kidding? We have just invested $10 million in your education. We are not about to let you go. Now get back to work!"

ONE MINUTE MESSAGE: We all fail, but we keep on going by the grace of God.

Egyptians Child Too

Amos 9:7-10

Fred Craddock reminded us of an old tale told by the Jewish rabbis. When it came time for the children of Israel to cross the Red Sea, God was busy and sent a group of angels to be in charge. As they were looking over the balcony of heaven, down upon earth, they divided the Red Sea, and the children of Israel crossed on dry land. As the water came rushing in, destroying some of the Egyptians, the angels began to rejoice. “We got ‘em, we got ‘em!”

The Almighty passed by and asked, “What’s going on?”

“We got ‘em! We got ‘em!”, the angels answered.

And God said, “You are dismissed from my service.”

They asked, “Why?”

And God said, “Don’t you know that the Egyptians are my children too?”

ONE MINUTE MESSAGE: God loves my best friend and my worst enemy as much as he loves me.

Kubelik

Matthew 7:9-12

William Barclay told the story of Evelyn Bell, who was a student of the violin. The famous violinist, Kubelik, was to give a concert in Queen's Hall in London. Her teacher gave her an introduction to Kubelik and she went to ask him for a ticket, since there were none to be had at the ticket office. Kubelik told her that he could do nothing; there was not room for a mouse in Queen's hall for that concert.

"What am I to do to about the concert?" she asked, almost weeping. "If I can't get a ticket, I will never hear you play."

"Oh, but you will!" said Kubelik. "Sit there!" And Kubelik played his concert program to an audience of one.

ONE MINUTE MESSAGE: No one is more valuable to God than you.

Bob Gunn

Psalms 57:1-5

Bob Gunn, a Methodist minister in Alabama and one of my favorite friends, told the story of once visiting in a home that had just suffered the death of a beautiful teenage daughter. She was brilliant and a wonderful Christian. She was in a tragic accident. He said to the mother, "How are you doing?"

And she said, "I'm angry! I'm angry! I'm so mad I don't know what to do, and I'm angry with God."

He said to her, "Well, why don't you tell him? He can take it."

ONE MINUTE MESSAGE: The best prayer is one of honesty.

D. L. Moody

1 Kings 19:9-13

Billy Graham told of the story when D.L. Moody once was invited to preach at New York's sophisticated Fifth Avenue Presbyterian Church. Many of its more intellectual parishioners didn't want him to, but he came anyway.

He decided to preach on Daniel, except he couldn't pronounce "Daniel," so he said "Danel." He had a high nasal twang, and he not only said "ain't," he said "hain't." At that time, Moody weighed 300 pounds, and his beard came almost to his eyes.

He lost his audience. People were embarrassed; some even snickered. But Moody kept on going.

About halfway through his sermon, people began to sit on the edge of their seats. They were no longer hearing Moody; they were listening to another voice, the voice of God.

ONE MINUTE MESSAGE: Are we listening to the still, small voice?

Waylon

Matthew 16:13-20

Dennis Foust told me a story related to him around a table in Fort Worth. Will Campbell, the author, told about conversations he had with Waylon Jennings, the country music singer. Will Campbell had sort of been the official unofficial pastor of Waylon Jennings and traveled with Jennings on some of his trips. He thought that he would talk to Waylon Jennings about his spiritual condition, and said "What do you believe about Jesus?"

Waylon said, "Uh-huh." That's it, that's all he said.

A few weeks later he thought he would ask again. "What do you believe about Jesus?"

Ole Waylon said, "Uh-huh" — a man of few words.

A few weeks later he decided he would ask again. "Let's elaborate on it, what do you believe about Jesus?"

Waylon said, "Well, let me ask you this All of the books that have been written about him, have they ever improved on Jesus?"

Will said, "No."

He said, "Well, then that's what I believe. I believe in Jesus."

ONE MINUTE MESSAGE: What do you believe about Jesus? Uh-huh!

Frederick II

Psalms 51:1-13

Lloyd Steffin wrote of a time in the eighteenth century when King Frederick II of Prussia visited a Berlin prison. One inmate after another tried to convince the monarch of their innocence. Amazing! To hear them tell it, they were all being unjustly punished for crimes they never committed — all, that is, except one man who sat quietly in a corner while all the rest unfolded their lengthy and complicated stories.

Seeing him sitting there, oblivious to the commotion, the king asked the man why he was in prison. "Armed robbery, your honor."

The king asked, "Were you guilty?"

"Yes sir," he answered, without attempting to excuse his wrongdoing.

King Frederick then gave the guard an order: "Release this guilty man. I don't want him corrupting all these innocent people."

ONE MINUTE MESSAGE: Confession is saying the same about our sin that God does.

Ask Me To Help

Mark 10:17-27

David J. Wolpe told the story when a boy and his father were walking along a road when they came across a large stone. The boy said to his father, "Do you think if I use all my strength, I can move this rock?"

"If you use all your strength, I am sure you can do it."

The boy began to push the rock. Exerting himself as much as he could, he pushed and pushed. The rock did not move. Discouraged, he said to his father, "You were wrong, I can't do it."

The father placed his arm around the boy's shoulder and said, "No, son, you didn't use all your strength — you didn't ask me to help."

ONE MINUTE MESSAGE: The impossible becomes possible when we use all our strength.

Not Steal An Apple

1 Corinthians 10:11-13

The story was told of a nine-year-old boy sitting on the fence beside the road, with his eye firmly fixed on the luscious red apples hanging on a nearby tree.

The farmer in the field noticed the young man from a distance. Realizing the situation, he quickly drove his tractor over to where the young boy was sitting. “Excuse me, young man,” he quizzed. “Are you trying to steal an apple?”

“No, sir,” the boy replied. “I am trying *not* to steal an apple.”

ONE MINUTE MESSAGE: “You cannot keep a bird from flying over your head, but you can keep him from building a nest in your hair.” *Martin Luther*

Two Brothers

1 John 4:7-21

William Bausch told the story of two brothers, one married and one single, who worked together on a family farm. They shared equally in work and profit.

One brother thought, "It is not right that we should share the profit equally. I am by myself, and my needs are simple. My brother has a wife and those children." So in the middle of the night he secretly took a sack of grain from his bin and dumped it in his brother's bin.

Meanwhile, unknown to him, his brother had the same thought. "I have my family, but my brother has no one. It is not right that we share equally." So he began to take a sack of grain each night and place it in his brother's bin.

As fate would have it, one night they bumped into each other in the dark, carrying their sacks. When it dawned on them what had happened, they each dropped their sacks and embraced.

ONE MINUTE MESSAGE: Where brothers and sisters dwell in love, therein is the presence of God.

Bob Hayes

Daniel 1:1-8

He was known as the world's fastest human and an all-pro wide receiver for the Dallas Cowboys. Before that, Bob Hayes was on the track team at the 1964 Tokyo Olympics where he had been clocked in the 100-yard-dash in 9.1 seconds, a world record.

It was at the Tokyo Olympics that Hayes was a member of the 440-relay team. Being the fastest, he was the anchor, or the last man to run. His team was the heavy favorite.

The race began, but on the second exchange, something went wrong. The baton was dropped, and the U. S. A. track team was hopelessly behind. But Bob Hayes had other ideas. When he finally got the baton, he ran the first 100-yards in 8.6 seconds — Humanly impossible?

Not to someone who had a purpose to win!

ONE MINUTE MESSAGE: God has a purpose for each one of our lives.

Wedding Gown

1 Chronicles 17:1-15

Did you notice this in a recent edition of "The Chattanooga Times"? On June 24, the following appeared in the want ads. In large print it read:

FOR SALE — WEDDING GOWN. NEVER USED.
SIZE 10. IVORY. COST NEW — $500.
ASKING — $225
(And then the ad quoted the telephone number)

Says a lot, doesn't it? Hope is lost. For whatever reason and possibly through no fault of her own, the dream is gone.

ONE MINUTE MESSAGE: Look for the healing hand of God to mend the broken dreams of your life.

Bad Decisions

Matthew 26:69-75

Tim Hansel told the story of a young man who had been elected to take over as bank president. He strode into the outgoing bank president's office and said, "Sir, I would like your advice. What will make me as successful as you?"

The older man looked up from his papers, eyed the young man up and down and rather curtly said, "Two words: Good decisions!"

The young man thanked the outgoing president and left the office. But then he turned, knocked on the door, and said, "Please forgive me for bothering you again, but how does a person know he's making good decisions?"

The bank president waited for a moment. Then going back to his work, he said, "One word: Experience!"

The young man nodded and turned to walk out. But before he reached the door, he stopped and turned around. "Yes?" said the outgoing president.

"Well," the young man asked, "how do I get that experience?"

The mentor replied, "Bad decisions!"

ONE MINUTE MESSAGE: Often the best teacher is found in the *School Of Hard Knocks.*

Balderson In Hell

Judges 16:23-31

John Balderson told the story of a man who woke up in the afterlife. Looking around, he saw a place of utter beauty and splendor. He thought to himself, "It could have been much worse."

Immediately his every desire, his every whim, was supplied. Everything he wanted, everything he even slightly desired, was attended to with great detail and immediacy. He was in paradise!

As the weeks and months went on, he began to sense a restlessness within himself. Nothing was denied. There was no rejection, everything was given. Finally in the frustration he was feeling, he went to one of the attendants and said, "You know, I'm sorry to complain. But I am not happy. I would just like to have something that I cannot have unless I earn it."

The attendant replied, "That is not possible."

The man then said, "If that is true, I would just as soon be in hell."

The attendant responded, "Just where do you think you are?"

ONE MINUTE MESSAGE: The happiness of incessant victory could be the essence of hell.

Abraham's Tent

Matthew 7:1-6

The Jewish rabbis used to tell the story when one day Abraham invited a beggar to his tent for a meal. When grace was being said, the man began to curse God, declaring he could not bear to hear his name.

Seized with indignation, Abraham drove the blasphemer away. When he was at his prayers that night, God said to him, "This man has cursed and reviled me for fifty years and yet I have given him food to eat every day. Could you not put up with him for a single meal?"

ONE MINUTE MESSAGE: Only God has the right and the proper information to judge.

Procrastinator's Club

1 Thessalonians 5:1-11

Have you heard about the Procrastinators' Club of America? According to a newspaper article, they claim to have a membership of over 500,000, although only about 35,000 have actually sent in the membership application. The others were going to, but decided to put it off.

One member thought to be sending Christmas cards early one year was expelled from the club. He was later reinstated, however, when they found out the cards were for the previous year.

Another man vowed to quit smoking. He knew it would be easy for him because he had put off starting smoking.

ONE MINUTE MESSAGE: You can put off making up your mind, but cannot put off making up your life.

Not For $10,000

John 12:1-11

James Stewart told a story of a nun. This lady had spent many years among the lepers in Africa, giving of herself, spending time with them, eating with them, and living with them. Day in and day out she had given her life to them to the point that she had contracted the disease herself. It was said that on a particular occasion, a group of "high society folks" were visiting the colony. One of those high society women saw the nun upon her knees, much in the posture of Mary, binding the horrible and repulsive wounds of a leper. The woman shrieked, "Ooh! I would not do that for $10,000!"

The nun looked up at her and replied, "I wouldn't either!"

ONE MINUTE MESSAGE: One never stands as tall as when one stoops to help another.

Daddy With Me

John 14:15-27

I heard once of a little boy whose ball went over into the yard next door, and the older boys refused to give it back to him. The little fellow came into the house dissolved in tears, and in order to teach him self-reliance, twice his father sent him back to retrieve it on his own. When it was obvious this was not working, the father said, "Okay, I want you to make one more run of it, except this time I'll go with you."

On hearing those words, the lad wiped his tears and squared his shoulders and marched out with a new spring in his step. He went straight up to his antagonists and said, "I want my ball, and this time you had better give it to me, for I brought my Daddy with me!"

ONE MINUTE MESSAGE: God is with us every step of the way.

Water In Milk

Romans 12:1-3

A country preacher once told the following story: One of many children, he grew up poor on a farm during the Depression. He grew up thinking his father liked water in his milk.

As the family would gather around the table for the evening meal, the father would come in from the barn with the freshly drawn milk. After sifting it through a piece of cloth, he would pour full glasses of milk around the table. The children first and then the mother were served.

After that, he went over to the sink, turned his back to the family, poured the last of the milk into his glass and filled it with water. It always looked as if he had a full glass.

It was many years, he said, before he realized the love and selfless action of the father who drank water in his milk.

ONE MINUTE MESSAGE: The essence of love is sacrifice.

John Hannah

Matthew 6:19-21

There are a lot of *big* things you could say about John. First of all, he was big! He stood over six feet tall and weighed over 300 pounds. *Sports Illustrated* called him the greatest offensive lineman in the history of professional football. Many folks in Alabama will tell you he is the best ever to carry the colors of the Crimson Tide. Many people here in Chattanooga at the Baylor School will say he wore the red and gray as few ever have.

But maybe the biggest thing you could say about John is that he took his professional football signing bonus and gave it away. He gave it to a home for homeless boys.

Big in size, big in ability, big in heart — Big John, Big John Hannah.

ONE MINUTE MESSAGE: You can often judge the size of a person by the size of their heart.

Roy Reigles

Matthew 9:9-13

In 1929, the Rose Bowl game was being played between California and Georgia Tech. The score was 7 to 6. California was winning on their home soil. Georgia Tech had the ball, threatening to score, needing only a safety or a field goal to win the game.

Suddenly, Georgia Tech fumbled. The captain of the California team, Roy Reigles, grabbed the fumble. Georgia Tech flew on him, battered him, and spun him around, but never did get him to the ground. He found a hole and raced through it as hard as he could go. There he was, out in the open, running with all his might for the goal posts. But there was a big problem: He was headed the wrong way! He had become disoriented, confused, and was running toward his own goal line. His teammates were yelling at him, "Stop, you're going the wrong direction! Turn around!"

The roar of the crowd drowned out their warnings and on he went. His own teammates were after him, and one of the more agile men caught him and dragged him down on his own one-yard line.

In vain, they tried three downs, and on the fourth down they had to kick. Georgia Tech broke through the line and blocked the punt, covered the ball in the end zone, got two points for a safety, and won the game. California lost the Rose Bowl game, 8 to 7, all because Roy Reigles had run the wrong direction. Roy Reigles was not the first or last to make that mistake.

ONE MINUTE MESSAGE: In apathy, ignorance or misguided zeal, we can lose another game — the game of life!

Hug

Romans 10:5-13

The man was on his way to the county fair. He had a chicken in one hand, a pig under his other arm, and a basket on his head. On the way, he became lost. As he tried to decide which direction to take, a lady passed by. "Excuse me, ma'am," he said, "can you tell me how to get to the county fair?"

She said, "I sure can. In fact, I'm going there myself, so we can just walk together." She explained, "We are going up this way a mile, and then left for a mile, and then left for about half a mile, and we'll be there."

"Wait a minute," interrupted the stranger. "Did you say we were going up this way a mile, then left for a mile, and then left for about half a mile?"

"That's right," she replied. The stranger made a suggestion. "Wouldn't it be quicker if we just cut through the woods?"

The lady protested, "I can't walk through the woods with you. You might try to hug me."

The man was stunned. "How in the world could I hug you? I have a chicken in one hand, a pig under the other arm, and a basket on my head?"

Without missing a beat, the lady returned, "You could put the chicken on the ground and put the basket over it, and I could hold that little bitty ole pig!"

ONE MINUTE MESSAGE: When you give a hug, you expose your most vulnerable area — your heart.

God Is Missing

Psalms 139:1-24

These two little boys were the terror of the school, into everything and constantly making one another laugh until their teacher had finally had it. So she sent the two miscreants to the principal's office for the umpteenth time.

The principal, who was also weary of seeing the two little devils time and time again, snatched one up by the arm, took him behind a closed door and put his shaking finger right on the kid's nose, and bellowed, "Where is God? Now you get back out there and think about that!"

The little boy, badly shaken, went back to the chairs outside the principal's office and his cohort, noticing how shaken his friend was, looked at him wide-eyed and asked what in the world just happened.

"God is missing and they think you and me had something to do with it!"

ONE MINUTE MESSAGE: The God you are looking for is already looking for you.

Lighthouse

Matthew 5:14-16

A large ship made its way through a dark and stormy night. It noticed in the distance two lights shining. It sent a message: "We are on a collision course. Alter your path ten degrees north."

The lights responded, "I order you to alter your course ten degrees south."

The ship's officer took the radio himself and said, "This is the admiral speaking, and this is a battleship. Alter your course ten degrees north and do it now! That's on order!"

There was a moment of silence, and then a timid voice responded. "Sir, I know that you are an admiral and I know that I am only a second lieutenant junior grade. I know that you are a battleship, but, sir, I am a lighthouse."

ONE MINUTE MESSAGE: Try to let the light of God shine on the inevitable obstacles of life.

Einstein And Chauffeur

Matthew 7:7-12

Brian Harbor told the following story. Albert Einstein was one of the most brilliant men who ever lived. His name has become synonymous with genius. Einstein also had a sense of humor. Like the time he was on a tour of universities explaining his theory of relativity. Since Einstein did not drive, he had to be chauffeured from place to place.

One day, on the way to another speaking engagement, the chauffeur said to Einstein, "You know, I've heard this lecture so many times now that I could give it myself."

Einstein responded, "Let's see. The people at the next university have never seen me before, so they don't know what I look like. Let me put on your uniform and cap, and you put on my clothes and introduce me as your chauffeur. Tell them that you are Dr. Einstein, and then you can deliver the speech."

After the speech, a mathematics professor asked a complicated, technical question involving mathematical formulas in technical language the chauffeur did not understand. The chauffeur responded, "Sir, the solution to that problem is so simple I am really surprised you would ask me to answer it. Anybody can answer it. In fact," he suggested, "I'm going to ask my chauffeur to come up here and answer it!"

ONE MINUTE MESSAGE: When you don't have all the answers, it's best to call on someone else.

Sir Francis Drake

2 Timothy 4:6-8

Many years ago, a young man from Devon, England left his hometown to join the fleet of Sir Francis Drake. Years later he came back and saw a friend that he had known before. The friend had become fat and lazy. The friend asked the man, "What have you to show for all your years upon the sea?"

The sailor was quite honest and he said, "Well, really not much to be honest with you. In fact, I often was cold and many times I was hungry, I was shipwrecked twice and many times I was scared half to death. But let me remind you, my friend, I sailed with the greatest captain who ever sailed the seas."

ONE MINUTE MESSAGE: In the greatest journey — life — who is your captain?

Tauler's Beggar

Psalms 100:1-5

The German mystic, Tauler, told the story that was quoted by Alistair McClean. Tauler was making a journey, and he came upon a beggar. He looked down at the beggar in his rags and filth, and he said, "Have a good day, my man."

The beggar responded, "I've never had a bad day."

"Well, then have a happy life."

The beggar responded, "I've never been unhappy."

"Oh? What do you mean?"

The beggar answered, "It is simple. If things are fine, I thank God. If things are not fine, I thank God. If I am filled, I thank God. If I am hungry, I thank God. For, you see, God's will is my will; and if God's will is my will, how can I ever be unhappy?"

Tauler looked at him again and said, "That is astonishing! Who are you?"

The beggar said, "I am a king."

"A king? You, a king? If you are a king, where is your kingdom?"

The beggar said, "In my heart, in my heart."

ONE MINUTE MESSAGE: One is about as happy as one makes up their mind to be.

Little Annie

1 Corinthians 13:1-13

Zig Ziglar told the story when a number a years ago, in a mental institution outside Boston, a young girl known as "Little Annie" was locked in a dungeon. Often attacking those who came around her, she was considered so "hopelessly insane" that she was assigned to a living death in a small cage.

An elderly nurse refused to accept that diagnosis and began to show love to "Little Annie." Often visiting her, once she left a plate of brownies beside her cage. Upon returning, the brownies were gone. After this, "Little Annie" began to improve until she was released from the cage and finally from the asylum. Then, she began to show the love that had been shown to her.

Many years later, Queen Victoria pinned England's highest honor upon Helen Keller. America's first Lady of Courage expanded, "I could not have accomplished anything without my teacher, Little Annie"... Annie Sullivan, the miracle worker.

ONE MINUTE MESSAGE: When love is patient and kind, the impossible becomes possible.

Wayne Oates

Psalms 68:3-4

Dr. Wayne Oates was one of my seminary professors. When he was a young graduate student, Wayne pastored a small church in Kentucky. He and his wife would commute to the church on Saturdays, hold services on Sundays, and return to the school Sunday evening. On one such occasion they were staying with an old farmer and his wife. After an early dinner, the old farmer and his wife washed the dishes. Then the farmer looked at the young pastor. "Brother Oates," he said, "are you or Mrs. Oates sick?"

Wayne responded, "Why, no, we're fine."

"Good," said the farmer. "If you was, me and the missus would sit up with you. Being how you ain't, we'll be going to bed." As the old couple started up the stairs, the farmer turned and said, "Make yourselves at home. You're welcome to anything we have. If there's anything you want and can't find, come up and wake us up — and we'll come down and teach you how to get along without it."

ONE MINUTE MESSAGE: Happiness is not having what we want, but appreciating what we have.

Know We Are Insane

1 Corinthians 8:1-13

Rabbi Abraham Hershell told a fable of a kingdom in which their entire harvest of grain was poisoned. Everyone who ate the grain became insane, and it brought about a crisis in the kingdom. The greatest of minds were gathered together to decide what to do. They were faced with two alternatives: either starve to death or become insane. Finally, the wise king said, "We will eat the grain and become insane, but we will set aside a small group that will eat a different diet and then there will be someone who knows that we are insane."

ONE MINUTE MESSAGE: God can make sense out of the nonsense of life.

James Garfield

Ephesians 4:29-32

Steve Brown told the story of a wealthy Ohio farmer who was approached by a young man named Jamie, asking for a job. Taylor, the farmer, hired him and allowed Jamie to sleep in the barn.

Over the ensuing weeks and months, Jamie proved to be a hard worker. One day, Jamie came to Taylor and announced that he and the wealthy man's daughter had fallen in love. The young worker asked Taylor for his daughter's hand in marriage. Taylor was incensed; he exclaimed, "I've treated you well and this is how you repay me! — Get your things and go!"

Jamie left and Taylor never heard from him again.

Years later, Taylor was cleaning in the barn and came to an area where Jamie used to sleep. There, when the straw was swept away, he was startled to find the place where Jamie had carved his full name in the wood. It read: James A. Garfield. Taylor was astounded to find that his undeserving farm hand had gone on to become a general and the President of the United States.

ONE MINUTE MESSAGE: Be kind to all. You never know who they will become.

Johnny Gave Blood

1 Peter 1:17-21

Myron Morris told the story about a little boy who was told by his doctor that he could save his sister's life by giving her blood. The six-year-old girl was near death, and her only chance of recovering was a blood transfusion from someone who had previously conquered the illness. Since the two children had the same rare blood type, the boy was the ideal donor.

"Johnny, would you give your blood for Mary?" the doctor asked.

The boy hesitated. His lower lip started to tremble. Then he smiled, "Sure, Doc, I'll give my blood for my sister."

Soon the two children were wheeled into the operating room. Mary, pale and thin and Johnny, robust and the picture of health. Neither spoke, but when their eyes met, Johnny grinned.

As his blood siphoned into Mary's veins, one could almost see new life come into her tired body. The ordeal was almost over when Johnny's little voice broke the silence. "Say, Doc, when do I die?"

It was only then that the doctor realized that little Johnny actually thought that in giving his blood to his sister, he was giving up his life.

ONE MINUTE MESSAGE: Remind you of anyone?

Carrier And McAllister

Matthew 6:9-15

Perhaps you saw on TV recently the story of Chris Carrier and David McAllister. Years ago, at the age of nine, Chris Carrier was kidnapped by a lone assailant, who not only kidnapped him but tortured him with burning cigarettes and shot him in the head, taking one of his eyes. He then abandoned him (a nine-year-old child) and he was found seven days later by a hunter.

Many years later, David McAllister was dying in a nursing home and he admitted that he was the one who abducted, tortured, and tried to kill Chris Carrier. When Chris heard that, he began visiting the nursing home every day to show mercy, love, and forgiveness. David McAllister, through dying lips said that Chris Carrier was the greatest friend he had ever had. You know what the clincher was? Chris Carrier, the one who forgave, the one who had been tortured, the one who was almost murdered said, "It must have been worse on him all these years than it was on me."

ONE MINUTE MESSAGE: Forgiveness begins when we realize that everyone has done wrong.

Colonel Parker

Galatians 6:7-9

Country singer Marty Robbins told the story of Elvis Presley's famous manager, Colonel Tom Parker. When he was young and getting started in the promotion business, Parker once went into a small Southern city and rented billboards. On these he put just two words — "IT'S COMING!"

Several weeks later he changed the ads to read — "IT'LL BE HERE DECEMBER 8, BUY YOUR TICKETS NOW."

Many people purchased tickets and showed up at the town's community center on the stated night. Parker stepped onto stage to draw back the curtains which revealed a sign onstage, then got into his car and left town. The sign said, "IT'S GONE."

ONE MINUTE MESSAGE: Listen to the God who tells the truth about us, not to those who deceive.

Algonquin Woman

1 Corinthians 13:4-8

Annie Dillard told a story in her book, *Writing Life*, of an Algonquin woman. The small group in which woman had lived all died from starvation. She and her small child were the only ones to survive. All she had was a little bone knife. By the side of a frozen lake, she found a small cache and in that cache was one fish hook.

Facing starvation, not only of herself but her child also, she took that bone knife and cut a piece of flesh from her thigh and made fish bait. She caught a jack fish, fed herself and her child and retained some of the fish for bait. Months later, after a frozen winter in the most harsh of climates, she and the child emerged. She still carries to this day a scar on her hip.

ONE MINUTE MESSAGE: When you truly love, you do what is necessary.

Marx' Daughter

Matthew 6:9-13

All of her life, she was told that God was a myth and that religion was nonsense, a hindrance to the progress of the people. It is like a poison, her famous father said; it poisons the mind and causes you to depend upon psychological crutches that simply are not true.

All of her life, she was taught this false theology, until one day she heard her name. Of all places, she heard it while reading a simple prayer which read something like this:

"Our Father, which art in heaven, hallowed be thy name,"

After reading that simple prayer, she said, "If there really is a God like that, I can believe in him."

And she became a Christian — the daughter of Karl Marx.

ONE MINUTE MESSAGE: The God of love still calls our name.

Brother Lost

Luke 15:1-31

Several years ago, I was attending to our three small boys in a shopping mall. Our twins were particularly adventuresome that day. I was continually losing them in the large stores. As I looked around, I had lost one for about the fifth time (I don't even remember which twin it was). Finally in exasperation, I said to the other two boys, "Come on, let's go. I'm tired of trying to find him."

I then turned, took the eldest son's hand and started walking "as if" to leave the lost twin. His brother had not moved. Instead he stood there, his back to me, looking down the aisle where he had last seen his four-year-old brother. Again, I called, "Come on, son."

He moved not! I went around to look at him and looked into that little face. His lower lip was trembling, there was concern in his wrinkled forehead, and a tear trickling down his cheek. He wasn't going anywhere! You see, *his brother was lost!*

ONE MINUTE MESSAGE: In the family of God, we always look out for each other.

Woman's Stone

Hebrews 9:23-28

Jack Canfield and Mark Hanson told the story of a wise woman who was traveling in the mountains and found a precious stone in a stream. The next day, she met another traveler who was hungry, and the wise woman opened her bag to share her food. The hungry traveler saw the precious stone in the wise woman's bag, admired it, and asked the wise woman to give it to him. The wise woman did so without hesitation.

The traveler left, rejoicing in his good fortune. He knew the jewel was worth enough to give him security for the rest of his life.

But a few days later he came back, searching for the wise woman. When he found her, he returned the stone and said, "I have been thinking. I know how valuable this stone is, but I give it back to you in the hope that you can give me something much more precious. If you can, give me what you have within you that enabled you to give me the stone."

ONE MINUTE MESSAGE: I hope that you find what was in Jesus that enabled him to give his life for you.

Craddock Bar-B-Q

Acts 2:1-13

My mentor and friend, Fred Craddock, told of years ago when he served as pastor of a small congregation near Oak Ridge, Tennessee. Hordes of people began to move there because of the excitement and jobs associated with the utilization of atomic energy.

Every residence for rent was quickly taken. Fearful of the incoming masses, the church voted, over the protest of the pastor, that one had to be a property owner in the county to be a member of the church.

Years later, Dr. Craddock took his wife, Nettie, by the site of the church. The building was still there. So were the masses; Parthians, Medes, and Elamites, residents of Mesopotamia, Judea, Cappadocia, Pontus, and so on. Over the door of the church building was a sign which read, "Bar-B-Q!"

He remarked to his wife, "It's a good thing that this is a restaurant, because if it were still a church, all these people would not be welcome here."

ONE MINUTE MESSAGE: When we seek to exclude, we wind up excluding ourselves.

Slover

1 Peter 2:13-17

In 1990, Charles Slover, a Baptist deacon, was traveling by train from Seoul to Kumi, Korea, on business. The smoke-filled cabin was aggravating his lungs, so he moved to the platform outside the train car where others were gathered for a breath of fresh air. Slover tried to communicate with one of the Korean men, but unsuccessfully, because the man seemed to speak no English and Slover spoke no Korean. Both experienced frustration and confusion.

Having given up on finding a common word, the Korean then began to sing in clear English, "Amazing grace, how sweet the sound that saved a wretch like me."

Knowing nothing else to do, Slover joined the Korean in the rest of the first verse. Again, they tried to communicate, but to no avail. So, they sang another verse of "Amazing Grace."

Knowing nothing else to do, they shook hands, hugged each other as brothers in Christ and never saw each other again. But they will.

ONE MINUTE MESSAGE: God's love is a universal language.

Buying The Photo

Galatians 2:17-21

It is a true story they say; An elderly and very wealthy man died but he left no will. They had no idea what to do with his vast estate. They decided to have an auction. An elderly, wrinkled, and tired woman came to the auction. She shuffled through the bits of things to be auctioned off as if she were looking for something. She found a framed photograph of the wealthy man's son. He was born sickly and died at an early age. The elderly little lady had been his nurse. She loved the son and wanted something by which she could remember him.

She purchased, for a very small amount of money, the old and tattered framed photograph of the son. As she was walking away from the auction, she noticed that the old framed photograph was rather thick; and as she turned it over to look, she saw something bulging. As she opened it, she found the will of the man who died. His will simply read, "Everything I have belongs to the one who honors my son by buying this photograph."

ONE MINUTE MESSAGE: When we honor the son, we get everything else.

Morse Code

1 Samuel 3:1-9

Back when the telegraph was the fastest method of long-distance communication, a young man answered an ad in the newspaper for a job as a Morse code operator. When he arrived, the office was filled with other applicants. The office was busy with noise and clatter, including the sound of a telegraph in the background. He was instructed by the receptionist to fill out an application and wait until he was summoned to enter the inner office. The young man filled out his application and sat down to wait with the other applicants. After a few minutes, the young man stood up and walked into the inner office.

The other applicants wondered what was happening. Within a few minutes, the employer escorted the young man out of the inner office and announced that the job had just been filled. The other applicants began to protest. One spoke up and said, "Wait a minute, I don't understand. He was the last one to come in. We never had a chance."

The employer said, "I'm sorry, but all the time you've been sitting here, the telegraph has been ticking out the following message in Morse code: 'If you understand this message, come in. The job is yours.'"

ONE MINUTE MESSAGE: God is speaking all the time. Are you listening?

Grandma Minnie

2 Corinthians 12:1-10

They called her Grandma Minnie. She was born in Alaska of Eskimo parents. She had eight children, all of whom she delivered herself. She spent many years delivering babies. "Babies like my hands," she said. "They are inviting hands."

When her husband died, she moved to Fairbanks to fulfill one of her wishes to "hear some real preachers preaching." One day a missionary saw Grandma Minnie looking at an oatmeal box and picking out the letters "JESUS" from the different words. Grandma Minnie asked, "That's Jesus, isn't it?"

Grandma Minnie was born in 1860. She was born again in 1960. She was taught to read at the age of 106 and she went to be with her Lord Jesus at the young age of 117.

ONE MINUTE MESSAGE: Often God uses the most unlikely — to show his strength.

G. W. Carver

1 John 3:1-2

In January of 1921, George Washington Carver was asked to come to Washington DC, to appear before the Ways and Means Committee to explain his work with the peanut. Dressed in worn clothes, carrying a battered suitcase, he was not treated with respect. Because he was black, he was the last in a long line to testify. He waited three days. He was horrified that, as he made his way to the microphone, he was the subject of racial slurs and taunts by our nation's leaders!

Dr. Carver wrote in his biography that as he started to walk away, he thought, "Whatever they said of me, I knew I was a child of God. So, I said to myself inwardly, 'Almighty God, let me carry out your will.'"

He was given twenty minutes to speak. So enthralled were they by his discussion, the chairman rose and asked for an extension, so he could continue, which he did for one and three-quarters hours. They voted four more extensions and he spoke for several hours.

ONE MINUTE MESSAGE: Be faithful as a child of God and your voice will be heard.

Buster Fikes

1 Thessalonians 5:1-2

Steve Tondera was a layman who was elected president of the Alabama Baptist Convention. Once en route to chair an important meeting in Montgomery, he noticed a hitchhiker on the side of the road. Although he seldom did so, he stopped and gave the man a ride. The hitchhiker was dirty, unshaven, and added a certain "air" to the interior of the automobile.

"My name is Steve. What's yours?"

"My name is Buster!" And with that, Buster began to unfold his story. He had traveled to Detroit with grand dreams for his life there. For a while, things went well. Then the bottom fell out. The dream vanished. The loss of his job, the loss of a relationship, unpaid bills, and now he was returning home defeated and with only the dirty clothes on his back.

"I haven't had breakfast. Care to join me?" Steve asked.

"I could eat," replied Buster. And could he! Like he had not eaten in days!

Resuming their journey, Steve felt an inner twitch to talk about his faith. Buster listened intently. Again, the twitch moved Steve to say, "Why don't we pull over to the side of the road and pray?"

"I can't pray" replied Buster.

Steve said, "If God will listen to me, he will listen to you." With that, they stopped under an overpass and knelt down beside the car. Buster asked Jesus to come into his life.

They then continued their journey. As they arrived at his destination, Steve gave to him his business card and a twenty dollar bill. About three or four weeks later, Steve received a letter. It was from Buster's mother. She thanked him again and again for leading Buster to Christ.

The following Sunday, Buster had made a public profession of faith and was baptized in the small church his mother attended. It was an answer to her many years of prayer. "He had never been happier," she said. "This past Tuesday, of all things, Buster was backing the pickup truck out of the driveway when he was struck by an automobile. Buster was killed."

ONE MINUTE MESSAGE: It's never too late to respond to God's call — or is it?

Am I Your Servant?

Mark 10:41-45

A southern pastor told of his church turning their parking lot into an outdoor skating rink for inner-city children in the '60s. As he stood with pride and watched the children glide on new skates, he felt a tug at his shirt. A small African American boy looked up at him and pointed to his untied shoelaces. "Okay, sure I'll tie your shoes," replied the pastor. A few moments later, he received another tug from the same little boy pointing to the other untied shoe. The pastor complied.

A moment or two later another tug occurred. It was the same little boy, but now the first one had come untied again. The pastor, looking down at the boy, said with exasperation, "Not you again! What do you think I am — your servant!?"

Catching his breath at his perspective, the pastor said to himself, "Yes, that's exactly what I am."

ONE MINUTE MESSAGE: The greatest of all is a servant.

Carter In Tuscumbia

1 Corinthians 15:50-57

In 1979, Jimmy Carter began his bid for re-election as President of the United States in Tuscumbia, Alabama, where I served as pastor of the First Baptist Church. The rally was held at Spring Park. Seventy thousand people crammed its boundaries. The most memorable thing about Carter's speech was the last three words, "We will win!"

Not even the President of the United States can always guarantee victory; but God can, because he has already won the victory through Jesus our Lord. Jesus has already conquered death, hell, and the grave for us.

ONE MINUTE MESSAGE: Because he lives, we shall live also.

Mets

Psalms 86:11-17

In 1969, the New York Mets won the World Series, becoming the world champions of baseball. Riding the strong arms of Jerry Koosman, Nolan Ryan, and "Terrific Tom" Seaver, the Mets beat the Baltimore Orioles. Many baseball experts considered the Baltimore Orioles to be the best team to come down the pike in years, but the Mets beat the Orioles in convincing fashion. Just a few years earlier, the New York Mets had set records for losing 120 games in a single year. They were called the "amazing Mets," because they found a new way to lose every day. They had been the epitome of futility, but in 1969 they won the World Series and earned the title the "Miracle Mets."

The headline in *Sports Illustrated* quoted the former Met manager Casey Stengel in his classic "Stengelese" when he said, "Who woulda thunk it?"

"Who woulda thunk" that the New York Mets would be World Series champions?

ONE MINUTE MESSAGE: The ways of God often catch us by surprise.

Hickman

Matthew 4:12-17

It was later attributed to a conversation between player Boyd Dowler and Coach Vince Lombardi of the Green Bay Packers, but I first read it in the *Herman Hickman Reader* authored by the same. Levi Jackson, a running back, played for Hickman when he coached football at Yale in 1949. One day a practice session was going horribly. The timing was off, the tackling was atrocious, and the blocking was worse.

Hickman called the squad together and said, "Everything is going wrong. We are going to start at the very bottom and work on fundamentals."

He held up a football for the squad to see and carefully and precisely explained, "This is a football."

Levi chirped in quickly and said, "Not so fast, coach, not so fast!"

ONE MINUTE MESSAGE: The basics of life rarely fail us.

Monks And Bread

2 Samuel 7:10-16

My good friend and mentor, Dr. Fred Craddock, told of when he was teaching a preaching class at the Candler School of Theology. Two Benedictine monks were members of his class. One of the monks returned on a Monday morning after a weekend visit to a monastery and told this story.

He said, "I spent the weekend at the Trappist Monastery in Conyers, Georgia, and a most marvelous thing happened to me. At mealtime, we were served the most delicious bread. It was wonderful! There was plenty of it. We were all enjoying it and no one was saying a word. As everyone was caught up in the moment of eating this delicious bread, I said to the brother seated next to me, 'Did we make this or did someone give it to us?'"

"And my brother responded, 'Yes.'"

ONE MINUTE MESSAGE: The interplay of human effort to divine favor is God's way.

Millard Fuller

2 Samuel 7:10-16

Millard Fuller, founder of Habitat for Humanity, preached in our sanctuary several years ago and told a story about one of their first blitz building efforts. I think it was in the early 1990s in North Carolina. Hundreds of people descended upon a particular area and blitzed-built a great number of houses in a week. One of the volunteers was former President of the United States, Jimmy Carter. President Carter worked on one house the entire week.

About two years later, Millard Fuller was taking some guests through this beautiful housing project built by Habitat. He drove down the street where Jimmy Carter had worked and stopped in front of the house upon which President Carter had helped build. There was a small boy playing in front of the house. Fuller asked boy, "Son, do you live around here?"

"Yes, sir, I live in that house right there," as he pointed to the house on which Jimmy Carter had worked.

Fuller said, "Let me ask you something, son. Do you know who built your house?"

The little boy said, "Yes sir, I know who built my house."

Fuller said, "Well then, tell me son, who built your house?"

The little boy responded, "God built my house!"

ONE MINUTE MESSAGE: Even when we build the house, God builds the house.

Miller's Orphan

Romans 15:1-4

Keith Miller tells of attending a small group session where Alice told her story. "When I was a tiny girl, I was put in an orphanage. I was not pretty at all, and no one wanted me. But I can recall longing to be adopted and loved by a family as far back as I can remember. But everything I did seemed to go wrong. I tried too hard to please everybody who came to look me over and all I did was drive people away. Then one day, the head of the orphanage told me a family was going to come and take me home with them. I was so excited I jumped up and down and cried. The matron reminded me that I was on trial and that it might not be a permanent arrangement. So, I went with this family and started school in their town – as a very happy little girl. And life began to open up for me, just a little."

"But one day, a few months later, I skipped home from school and ran in the front door of the big old house we lived in. No one was home, but there in the middle of the front hall was my battered old suitcase with my little coat thrown over it. As I stood there and looked at that suitcase, it slowly dawned on me what it meant — they didn't want me, and I hadn't even suspected."

Alice stopped speaking a moment, but Miller didn't notice. He and the rest of the group were standing in that front hall with the high ceiling, looking at the battered suitcase and trying not to cry. Then Alice cleared her throat and said almost matter-of-factly, "That happened to me seven times before I was thirteen years old."

Miller said that as he looked at this tall, forty-year-old, gray-haired woman, he wept. She looked up, surprised and touched that her story had elicited such a response. She held up her hand and shook her head slightly, in a gesture to stop them from feeling sorry for her. "Don't," she said with a genuinely happy smile, "I needed my past — it brought me to God."

ONE MINUTE MESSAGE: Kris Kristofferson said, "I have a great future in my past."

Behanna's Prayer

Romans 8:28-30

In 1967, I was privileged to hear Gert Behanna give her testimony to the pastor's conference of the Southern Baptist Convention in Miami, Florida. She chronicled her life as an alcoholic through failed marriages and the disappearance of a child. She met Christ late in life and possessed one of the most vibrant testimonies I have ever heard. When she concluded, 17,000 gave to her a standing ovation which seemed to last five minutes. She concluded with a paraphrase of the old slaves' prayer:

Lord, I ain't what I ought to be.
Lord, I ain't even what I could be.
But thank you, Lord, I ain't what I used to be.

ONE MINUTE MESSAGE: It's a joyful and sometimes bumpy road to Christlikeness.

Bob Oiler

Philippians 4:4-7

"There is no God!" he blatantly shouted. He would cross his arms and scream up into heaven, "If there is a God, let him strike me dead!" Then he would wait defiantly for that which he knew would not happen. Bob was the crudest, most profane, and distasteful person I had ever met. I met him in my third summer in the Republic Steel Mill in Gadsden, Alabama, working to earn money to go back to college to study for the ministry. And, oh, when he found out I was a young preacher…!

"Preachers are all liars," he spouted. "They all are just after your money. I don't believe in an educated preacher," he spewed about three inches from my face. For a man who said he did not believe in God, he sure used God's name a lot. But, if one could wade through all that venom and vengeance spurting from his foul mouth, one would find that he probably believed in God as much as anyone. He was just mad.

Years before, he had been a church person. Then his little daughter, his only daughter, had burned to death in a fire. He needed to make peace with God.

ONE MINUTE MESSAGE: Only God can give us lasting peace.

Church Used To Go

Romans 7:14-25

You may have heard the story of the man who was rescued from a deserted island after many years of isolation. “What did you do all those years?” the reporter asked.

“Well, I hunted, fished, and built those three buildings.”

“What are those buildings for?” the reporter pursued.

“One is my house and the other is my church,” replied the rescued man.

“What is the purpose of the third building?” the writer asked.

“Oh, nothing!” the man replied.

“Nothing?” the reporter asked.

“Well, if you must know,” the man replied, “that is the church I used to attend.”

ONE MINUTE MESSAGE: Often our greatest conflict is with ourselves.

Guadalcanal

Mark 10:17-22

I identify with the story told by Halford Luccock, recorded in *The New York Times* in an article by A.B.C. Whipple. There was, in Australia during the 1930s, a scholar of world events who foresaw that a great war was sure to break out. He realized that Japan would be one of the belligerents. Accordingly, this twentieth-century wise man studied the atlas in search of the perfect hiding place, the best possible island of escape from the storm about to break across the civilized world.

By the employment of careful logic and the process of deduction, he finally selected the spot, an obscure, virtually uninhabited island, and in the summer of 1939, he went ashore there.

The name of the island was Guadalcanal!

ONE MINUTE MESSAGE: We will travel far in an effort to escape ourselves.

Hawthorne

Acts 9:26-31

Nat came home from work, thoroughly discouraged by being fired from his job at the custom house. Most distressing was his task of telling his wife Sophia. Her reaction took him by complete surprise. With an exclamation of joy, she said, "Now you can write your book."

"Sure," he said, "and what will we live on while I'm writing it?"

To his amazement, she opened a drawer and pulled out a substantial sum of money. "Where on earth did you get that?" he exclaimed.

"I have always known you were a man of genius," she told him. "I knew that someday you would write a masterpiece. So, every week, out of the money you gave me for housekeeping, I saved a little bit. So, here is enough to last us for a whole year."

So, Nat wrote his novel. Nat — Nathaniel Hawthorne, who wrote *The Scarlet Letter!*

ONE MINUTE MESSAGE: God often works through the encouragement of others.

Rossetti

Luke 18:1-8

Dante Gabriel Rossetti, the famous nineteenth-century poet and artist, was once approached by an elderly man. The old fellow had some sketches and drawings that he wanted Rossetti to look at and tell him if they were any good, or if they at least showed potential talent. Rossetti looked them over carefully. After the first few, he knew that they were worthless, showing not the least sign of artistic talent. But Rossetti was a kind man, and he told the elderly man as gently as possible that the pictures were without much value and showed little talent. He was sorry, but he could not lie to the man.

The visitor was disappointed but, seemed to expect Rossetti's judgment. He then apologized for taking up Rossetti's time, but asked that he just look at a few more drawings — these done by a young art student? Rossetti looked over the second batch of sketches and immediately became enthusiastic over the talent they revealed. "These," he said, "Oh, these are good. This young student has great talent. He should be given every help and encouragement in his career as an artist. He has a great future if he will work hard and stick to it."

Rossetti could see that the old fellow was deeply moved. "Who is this fine young artist?" he asked. "Your son?"

"No, "said the old man sadly. "It was me, forty years ago. If only I had heard your praise then! I got discouraged and gave up too soon."

ONE MINUTE MESSAGE: Winston Churchill's most famous speech consisted of four words, "Never, never give up!"

Grandpa's Letter

2 Timothy 1:8-13

For most of my fifty years in the ministry, I have had people ask me, "Are you any relation to that old Preacher Carver who used to preach around Arab, Alabama?"

"Yes, I am proud to say that he was my grandfather." My response then would bring the litany of stories about how my grandfather had touched their lives through encouragement. One such person was Roland Clemons approached me at a state convention meeting. "I was picking cotton," he said, "with your grandparents. I turned to the old man and said, 'Preacher Frank, I think that God is calling me into the ministry.'"

"Are you sure?" my grandfather asked.

"I think so," Clemons responded.

"Well, son, put down that pick sack right now and get to it!"

"I lived with them for months," he said. "That old man would sit up most of the night talking Bible and then plow all the next day. He was my seminary before I went to seminary."

In 1964, on the day before I entered college, we buried my grandfather. In the church he built with his own hands, his funeral service was conducted by six ministers, all of whom he had helped to start in the ministry. Seven, if you include his son. Eight if you include me.

I still have in my office the last postcard he wrote to me. In shaky script the concluding words were, "I have prayed that it be God's will for me to hear you preach God's word." He died within two weeks.

I entered the ministry thirteen months later. God did not answer his prayer. Grandpa has never heard me preach. Or has he?

ONE MINUTE MESSAGE: God has many choice servants issuing his call.

Mirror

1 Corinthians 13:9-12

You may have heard the story about the preacher who stopped by his church one afternoon while the building was in the process of being redecorated. As he wandered through the building, darkness came before he realized. All of a sudden he found himself in a room with which he was unfamiliar. The door shut behind him. He tried the door, to find no doorknob on the inside. It was dark and he began to panic. No one was around — no staff, no builders, no custodian! He waited for a moment so that his eyes could adjust to the darkness. Suddenly he turned and saw the figure of another man. He was frightened, but he regained his composure and said, "What are you doing here?"

The man did not respond. He thought the man looked like him, only bigger, meaner looking, and ugly. He asked again, "What are you doing here?" Again, the figure of the man did not respond.

Just as he was about to strike out against the ugly man, his eyes better adjusted to the darkness and he found himself facing a mirror!

ONE MINUTE MESSAGE: When our own self-image is distorted, we often strike out at others.

Charles Merrill

Psalms 119:18

Dudley Rose was the Charles E. Merrill Fellowship advisor at Harvard. He told the story of a time he was called on the telephone by a bookstore clerk. "I have an old man in the store rummaging through some old books who says that you will verify his check. He is shabbily dressed and says his name is 'Mara' or 'Morrow' or something like that."

Dudley responded, "Is this man tall, slender, and gray headed?"

"Yeah!" the clerk said, "believe he is!"

"Listen, my friend," Dudley continued, "if he offers you a check for the books, take it! If he offers you a check for the building, take it! Ever heard of Merrill-Lynch?"

ONE MINUTE MESSAGE: Things are not always what or who they seem.

Tampling

Matthew 25:14-30

Andy Tampling and his wife began their ministry in a small church in northern Florida. The first Sunday he was in the pulpit, a white boutonniere appeared with his name on it. He put it on. Every Sunday the white boutonniere was there. Wearing a white boutonniere became his trademark. He had no idea who was sending it. He and his wife would often sit over a cup of coffee and imagine who in the church was doing that. They went to the florist and asked who was sending it. The florist said, "It's paid for in cash, and they wish to remain anonymous."

As he moved from that church to the First Baptist Church of Opp, Alabama, the flower was there in the pulpit as before. "Well, whoever it is, they are sending it from Florida." They again would talk, "Well, it could be…?"

Years later they moved to the First Baptist Church of Sylacauga, Alabama, and the flower was on the pulpit the first Sunday and every Sunday thereafter. They would discuss it. "Well, I think it is…"

"No, she died. It can't be her. It has to be someone else."

He asked others. No one knew! The florist would not say a word. He then accepted a call to serve the First Baptist Church of Birmingham. The flower was sent anonymously every Sunday.

After seventeen years of pastoral ministry, Andy resigned to head up the Department of Retirement Centers for the State Convention. The second Sunday out of the pastorate, he was preaching a supply sermon in a church in Montgomery. As he and his wife were about to walk into the sanctuary, she turned to him and said, "This is difficult for you, isn't it?"

He agreed, "Yes, it is."

She said, "This is the first Sunday in seventeen years that you have not had a church. And then she said, "I'm sorry that I forgot to order your flower."

ONE MINUTE MESSAGE: It's the little stuff that counts.

Bloody Handkerchief

Revelation 7:9-14

When I was twelve years old, I pitched little league baseball. I was not very good, but my ineptitude was not due to a lack of encouragement from my father. The distance from the pitcher's mound and home plate was marked off in our driveway. Almost every day we would practice pitching. I would practice my only pitch, a fast ball and he would serve as my catcher. You ought to be aware that my father worked in the steel mill for over forty years. The constant exposure to the harsh detergents to remove the grease, coupled with an inherited skin disease often caused the skin on his hand to break open. He always used a handkerchief in the glove to soften the blow of my errant throws. "Throw it as hard as you can," he would shout. "You can throw harder than that."

I remember one day as we finished our practice, he put his arm around me and said, "You had a good arm today. You really threw hard."

He gave me his glove as he quickly put his white handkerchief in his pocket — the handkerchief that he had placed in his glove — the handkerchief with the fresh blood stains on it!

ONE MINUTE MESSAGE: Remind you of another who shed his blood for you?

Ralph Archbold

John 11:17-26

Jack Canfield told the story of Ralph Archbold, who delivered talks dressed in the character of Benjamin Franklin. He has been doing this for about twenty years in and around the Philadelphia area. Recently, he spoke at an elementary school assembly program, and after the program he was invited to visit a fifth grade class that was studying American history.

As Archbold, dressed in the character of Benjamin Franklin fielded questions, one of the students made the remark, "I thought you were dead."

Ralph Archbold said, "Well, I did die on April 19, 1790, at the age of 84, but I didn't like that very much, and I just decided I am never going to do it again."

A boy in the back of the class raised his hand and asked, "When you were in heaven, did you see my mother?"

Archbold said, "My heart almost stopped. I wanted the floor to open up and swallow me. My only thought was, 'Don't blow this!'"

Archbold said, "It was as if some divine word was given to me and I heard my voice saying, 'Well, I don't know if she was the one I think she was, but if she was, she was the most beautiful angel there.'"

The boy's face beamed and that told me that I gave the right answer.

ONE MINUTE MESSAGE: We all are terminal.

University Of Louisville

2 Timothy 4:1-2

The University of Louisville Cardinal basketball team went to a tournament several years ago in Hawaii. At their first practice session in Maui, they discovered that the managers had forgotten to bring basketballs. They looked around in dismay and then heard a basketball bouncing outside the gym. They saw a young lad with an old battered, well-worn basketball. They tried to buy the basketball from the young man. "Ten dollars?" "No!"

"Fifteen dollars? Twenty-five dollars? Fifty dollars?"

"No! I'll not sell my basketball."

In the meantime, one of the Cardinal players said to the little boy, "You know, fellow, you're dumb. You could have sold that basketball for fifty dollars."

The little boy scratched his nose and said, "Well, mister, I may be dumb. But at least I'm smart enough to know that if you're going to practice basketball, you need to bring a basketball!"

ONE MINUTE MESSAGE: Are you prepared for whatever?

French Soldiers

John 10:11-18

Shell-shocked soldiers presented a perplexing problem for the French Army following the conclusion of World War I. So shell-shocked were such soldiers, over 100 in number, that they had amnesia. They could not remember their own names. They were healthy in every other way, ready to return home to their families, but they could not remember their own identity. The French Army, due to a faulty record-keeping system, did not know who they were either. Perplexing problem!

It was suggested that the French Army hold an identification rally in an effort to name these homeless heroes. After invitations to would-be families had been sent, interested parties were gathered in a large plaza in Paris. One by one, these amnesia-ridden victims made their way to the microphone and pleaded, "Can anyone out there please tell me who I am? Can you please tell me my name?"

Reporters gathered for the rally stated that few events in the entire war rivaled this one for its sheer drama.

ONE MINUTE MESSAGE: God knows your name.

One Heartbeat

Luke 12:13-21

The morning was not far spent when the weary pastor made her way across the hospital parking lot. The night had been long as she prayed with, comforted, and then tried to console a young couple as their small child left this world for the loving hands of its heavenly Father.

Her heart was heavy with things eternal when she almost bumped into a mother and her small daughter. "Please forgive me, I'm sorry," she said as she sought to be on her way.

"I know you," the little girl declared. "Aren't you that preacher? Aren't you the preacher in that big red church?"

"Why, yes, honey I am," the pastor responded.

"Tell me something, preacher," she said. "Where is heaven?"

"I beg your pardon?"

"Heaven, how far away is heaven?" the little girl asked.

"Let's see, honey, place your hand over your chest and tell me what you feel."

"My heartbeat," she responded. "I feel my heartbeat!"

"That's just how far away heaven is, honey," the pastor responded, "one single heartbeat!"

ONE MINUTE MESSAGE: The best way to prepare for tomorrow is to live fully today.

Steve Sloan

Acts 11:19-26

He was Wiseman of America's number one high school quarterback. He was the Associated Press' number one high school football and basketball player in America during 1961. He signed a college football scholarship to play for the legendary Paul "Bear" Bryant at the University of Alabama, where he was the starting quarterback in three major bowl games. He was chosen All-American, the "Most Valuable Player" in the 1966 Orange Bowl, Atlanta Touchdown Club's Most Valuable Player in the Southeastern Conference 1965, and winner of the Sammy Baugh Trophy presented by the Columbus, Ohio, Touchdown Club, 1965. But Steve Sloan later stated that the greatest honor he ever received was from a less-than-friendly student who pushed him aside while passing him on his college campus and said, "Get out of the way, Christian!"

The greatest honor he ever received was to be called Christian — a child of God.

ONE MINUTE MESSAGE: We will never receive a greater honor than to be called a Christian, nor one that we deserve less.

Chris Wren

2 Corinthians 9:12-15

In 1666, the great fire of London destroyed much of the city. Christopher Wren was chosen to serve as the major architect to rebuild the city from the rubbish. His greatest challenge was to be the architect for the rebuilding of Saint Paul's Cathedral, a task at which he spent 35 years of his life. When the project was completed, the reigning monarch of the day, Queen Ann, was given a guided tour of the edifice by Christopher Wren. When she viewed the structure upon which he had given the major effort of his life's work, she remarked, "It is awful; it is artificial; it is amusing."

Now what if someone had made those comments about a work upon which you had spent 35 years? You and I might be devastated. Christopher Wren gave a huge sigh of relief, and said, "Thank you, your majesty," and bowed at her feet.

Why? Because in seventeenth-century England, those words had different meanings than they have today. In those days, "awful" meant awe-inspiring, "artificial" meant artistic, and "amusing" meant amazing. No wonder Wren was pleased. Queen Ann was giving to him the highest compliment of his time. There are those who have seen it who say that even her words did not do justice to the work of Sir Christopher Wren.

ONE MINUTE MESSAGE: Some things are only describable through experience.

Ali

1 Samuel 15:1-11

Muhammed Ali was a three-time world heavyweight boxing champion. His face has appeared on the cover of *Sports Illustrated* more times than any other athlete. Some have tabbed him as the greatest athlete of the twentieth century. He has one of the most recognizable faces of anyone in the world. When he was "floating like a butterfly and stinging like a bee", he was king of the sports world. His entourage followed him around the globe.

Gary Smith, a reporter, went to see Ali. Ali escorted him out to a barn next to his farmhouse. On the floor, leaning against the walls, were mementos of Ali in his heyday. Photos were endless of his sculpted body, at its prime performing seemingly the impossible — the knockout of George Foreman — the "thrilla in Manilla."

On one the photos were white streaks — bird droppings. For some reason, Ali walked over to the photos and turned them one by one toward the wall. Then he walked to the barn door, stared at the countryside, and mumbled something. The reporter did not hear what he was saying, and he asked him to repeat it. Ali said, "I had the world, and it wasn't nothin'. Look now."

ONE MINUTE MESSAGE: The accolades of the world are fleeting.

God Take Picture

Hebrews 12:1-2

Tony Campolo told the story of his neighbor's four-year-old daughter. He said that if you put her in a Shirley Temple look-alike contest, she would win every time. One night, after her parents put her to bed, there arose a tremendous thunderstorm. The lightning was flashing all around, the thunder was making a loud rolling noise, and the wind was blowing the rain against the windows. The father ran upstairs to check on his daughter. "Honey, are you all right?" As he opened the door, she was standing up against the window spread out like an eagle. "Honey, what are you doing?"

She turned around with a great big smile on her face and said, "God is trying to take my picture!"

ONE MINUTE MESSAGE: We can interpret every event of life through the love and grace of God.

Grandpa Boyles

James 2:20-26

He was the kindest, gentlest, and quietest man I ever knew. Although I was around him a lot, I remember very little of anything he ever said. I do remember him sitting behind a blazing bowl of Carter Hall and quietly reading his Bible. Although he was the last person in the world you would picture doing so, a painter by trade, he was put in charge of a group of German prisoners of war during World War I. It was his job to plan their work and see to it that they accomplished it. Can you imagine a more difficult task?

But he performed his job with such integrity and kindness that they called him "Pops." Prisoners of war called him "Pops"! Now this happened not in Northern Africa or Europe, but in Huntsville, Alabama. That man was my maternal grandfather. Not my paternal grandfather. Not the one who was a preacher, or was he?

ONE MINUTE MESSAGE: We can show God's kindness anywhere.

Christ In My Son

Romans 9:28-30

William Bausch told the story of a mother realizing that two families in their neighborhood were experiencing difficulty, who told her children, "Don't give your father and me anything. Let's try to see that these families have a decent Christmas."

One son, Chris, was the basketball manager at his college and was in and out most of the time. In one of his brief visits, as he was walking out the door, he pressed into his mother's hand some money and said, "Take this. It is for those families so they can have a better Christmas."

As he bounded out the door, she saw a crisp fifty-dollar bill. Aware of the immense sacrifice it took for him to save that amount, she ran after him and jumped into his car. She hugged him. Then for a moment, she was not sitting next to her twenty-year-old son, but next to that same son at age five who forgave a friend for stealing his toy car. He said, "Better let me go, Mom, before I start to cry."

The mother said, "I love you, honey, and God will bless you for this."

"And with that," she said, "I climbed out of the car, leaving with a moment I shall cherish forever; the moment I saw Christ in my son."

ONE MINUTE MESSAGE: God gives the best gift — himself!

Lewis Grizzard

Colossians 3:12-14

Lewis Grizzard related a story that occurred at the Moreland Methodist Church in which he was reared. On Sunday nights they had a meeting called MYF (Methodist Youth Fellowship). He said that there were two rough boys, juvenile offenders in their community who had gotten into trouble. Their punishment, as designated by the court, was to go to MYF on Sunday nights for six months. That was their punishment!

Grizzard said that the first Sunday night they were there, they beat up two fifth graders and threw a Cokesbury hymnal at the woman who was in charge of the group and had brought cookies. She looked them square in the face and said, "I do not for one minute agree with what you did, and Jesus does not either, but I guess if Jesus can forgive you, I can too. Sit down, shut up, and eat a cookie!"

Grizzard said, "That was the day I saw my first miracle. The last I heard, both those boys had fine families, good jobs, and rarely missed a Sunday."

ONE MINUTE MESSAGE: Miracles happen all around us.

Want A Monkey

Romans 3:21-26

Several years ago, my wife wanted a monkey. I said, "What are you going to do with a monkey? We don't need a monkey."

"Yeah, I want a monkey," she said.

"Well, if you get a monkey, where will the monkey eat?"

"The monkey will eat with us."

"We don't need a monkey. Where will the monkey sleep?"

"Well, the monkey will sleep with us."

"We don't need a monkey. What about the odor?"

She said, "Well, I got used to it, so I guess the monkey can too."

ONE MINUTE MESSAGE: What truly binds us together is the fact that we are all sinners.

Belmont Abbey

Galatians 5:1-6

Robert Beringer told the story of Belmont Abbey College in North Carolina, that sits on property that was once a large southern plantation. The land was given to the Roman Catholic Church and they built an abbey and college on the property. The monks found a huge granite stone on the property upon which men, women, and children had stood centuries ago and were sold as slaves. The monks took the stone and hollowed out a hole in the top and carried it into the abbey's chapel, where to this day it serves as a baptismal font. The engraving on it reads: "Upon this rock men were once sold into slavery. Now upon this rock, through the water of baptism, people become free children of God."

ONE MINUTE MESSAGE: God's freedom brings corresponding responsibility.

Lincoln And Girl

Galatians 3:26-29

Dr. Stephen Brown related the following story: When Abraham Lincoln went to the slave market once, he was moved with compassion to place a bid on a young, black girl. He won the bid and walked away with his "property." There was a sullen, angry expression on the black girl's face, because she felt that here was another white man who had bought her and would abuse her. As they walked away from the slave block, Lincoln told the girl. "You are free."

"What does that mean?" she demanded.

"It means you are free."

"Does it mean that I can be what I want to be?" she asked.

"Yes," replied Lincoln, "you can be what you want to be."

"Does it mean I can say what I want to say?" she asked, her anger softening.

"Yes," Lincoln answered, "you can say what you want to say."

"Does it mean," she went on, "that I can go where I want to go?"

"Yes, you can go where you want to go "

"Then, "said the girl, "I will go with you."

ONE MINUTE MESSAGE: True freedom is to follow in the footprints of Jesus.

Miller's SS Member

Matthew 11:25-30

In his wonderful book, *Habitation of Dragons,* Keith Miller told the story of having lunch with a friend when an attractive young woman sauntered up to his table in a pair of very short shorts, sandals, and a brief halter top. She was followed by a tiny daughter in a similar outfit. Miller recognized the child as a member of the Sunday school class he taught. After a few moments of conversation the young woman remarked, "I would honestly like to make a commitment of my life to Christ… but I can't do it. I have a personal problem I can't resolve."

Miller responded, "That is why Christianity is called good news. God gives us the power to cope with the seemingly impossible situations in life. I can't promise to change anything… just accept his love and grace. We come to him as we are."

"Do you believe that?" she asked.

"I'd bet my life on it," Miller replied.

She looked at her hands for several minutes. "All right," she said, almost as a challenge. "I'm committing adultery every Thursday night with a man who has a wife and several children. And I cannot quit. Now can I come into your Christian family?"

ONE MINUTE MESSAGE: The church is open to all or none.

Boy And Candy

Proverbs 3:5-6

I was in a shopping mall a few years ago, talking with a four-year-old African American boy who was as cute as a speckled pup. We were having a big time passing the time while his mother and my wife shopped. I would grin at him and he would grin at me. I would wave at him and he would wave at me. I would laugh and he would laugh back. We were having the best time. I reached into my pocket, took out one of those little mints that I always carry and tried to give him one. No! No! He backed off. He would not take my candy.

On the way home, I sorrowfully told my wife that he would not take the candy. She said, "He has been taught not to trust strangers."

I said, "I'm no stranger, I'm me."

She said, "Believe me, you are stranger than you think."

ONE MINUTE MESSAGE: God can be trusted.

Peanuts

Mark 10:17-22

Do you remember the classic *Peanuts* cartoon in which Lucy was down and out, feeling despondent, in her usual foul mood? "I feel terrible!" she said.

Linus said, "Well, if you would only do…"

"I am not going to do that," she snapped.

"If you only would…" he responded.

"I'm not going to do that either," she retorted.

Linus responded with exasperation, "How in the world do you expect to feel better if you don't do something?"

She blared, "You don't understand. I don't want to feel better!"

ONE MINUTE MESSAGE: A rut can be a grave if we don't choose a way out.

Bishop Notre Dame

Acts 9:1-9

William J. Bausch discussed a story told by the man who served as the Bishop of Notre Dame in the early part of the 1900s. A young man stood outside the cathedral and shouted derogatory slogans at the people entering to worship. He would call them fools and all kinds of names. The people tried to ignore him, but it was difficult.

One day the parish priest went outside to confront the young man, much to the distress of the parishioners. The young man ranted and raved against everything the priest told him. Finally, he addressed the young scoffer by saying, "Look, let's get this over with once and for all. I'm going to dare you to do something and I bet you can't do it."

The young man shot back, "I can do anything you propose, you white-robed wimp!"

"Fine," said the priest. "All I ask you to do is to come into the sanctuary with me. I want you to stare at the figure of Christ, and I want you to scream at the very top of your lungs, as loudly as you can, 'Christ died on the cross for me and I don't care one bit.'"

So the young man went into the sanctuary and screamed as loud as he could, looking at the figure, "Christ died on the cross for me and I don't care one bit!"

The priest said, "Very good. Now do it again."

And again the young man screamed, with a little more hesitancy, "Christ died on the cross for me and I don't care one bit!"

"You're almost done now," said the priest. "One more time."

The young man raised his fist, kept looking at the statue, but the words wouldn't come. He just could not look at the face of Christ and say those words again. The Bishop continued, "I was that young man."

ONE MINUTE MESSAGE: In the face of love, harsh words are hard.

D. E. King

Matthew 6:19-21

When I was a student at the Southern Baptist Theological Seminary in Louisville, Kentucky, one of our finest chapel speakers was D.E. King, an African American preacher from Chicago. Someone asked Pastor King why black Christians were always so joyful in their worship, even when things were not going well. The pastor exclaimed, “We rejoice in what we are going to have.”

ONE MINUTE MESSAGE: We can rejoice, as Christians, in what we are going to be — like Jesus.

Jan Douglass

Revelation 7:9-17

His name was Jan Douglass. Two years before, he had pitched his team to the Little League World Series in Williamsport, Pennsylvania, where they placed third in the world. As he was taking the mound as our starting pitcher on July 4, 1960. We were playing for the Gadsden Pony League City Championship in a game that received press in *The Gadsden Times* twenty-five years later. Both teams sported identical 19-1 records. Douglass' only defeat was to his mound opponent that day, Macky Moates, in a crushing 12-3 shellacking. Over 10,000 fans crowded the ballpark, standing four deep around the outfield fence. As the visiting team, we were first at bat and unexplainedly scored four runs without the benefit of a hit. Before he threw a pitch, Douglass gathered the entire team around him as we took the field for the bottom half of the first inning. Jan said, "When the game is over, we are going to carry Coach Gallager around the bases."

To him, turn out the lights, the party was over! School was out! The game was won! And it was. He also clouted a mammoth home run just to accent his prediction. Oh, the other team scored a few runs, but to Jan Douglass, we were already city champions.

ONE MINUTE MESSAGE: With God, the eventual outcome is secure.

Troy Morrison

Jeremiah 10:5-10

For many years, Troy Morrison was the executive director of the Alabama Baptist State Convention. Prior to that, he served as the pastor of the Twelfth Street Baptist Church in Gadsden for seventeen years. During his pastorate there, he was once approached by a member of his congregation who asked, "Pastor, if ever anything happens to me, would you see that my children are cared for?"

He, like most pastors in such an awkward moment, responded, "Well, of course I would."

Within two years, the mother and the father both had died. Troy and his wife prayed and decided that they would honor his word to take care of the woman's children — all four of them, two of which were teenagers. There also were matters of a large hospital bill and funeral home bill for the mother's service. Word circulated about the Morrison's generous gesture.

Within a few days, Troy received a letter in the mail from the president of the Baptist Hospital. Enclosed was the mother's hospital bill. Across the bottom it read, "Paid in full!"

The next week, Dr. Morrison conducted a funeral service for another congregant. As he and the director of the Collier Butler Funeral Home were riding to the cemetery, the funeral director reached into his inside coat pocket, with tears in his eyes, and handed Troy an envelope. Inside the envelope was the mother's funeral bill. Across the bottom it read, "Paid in full!"

That is what Jesus did for us! He paid the price for our sins — in full!

ONE MINUTE MESSAGE: We all have a bill which someone else paid.

Football And My Father

Romans 8:1-4

For my senior year, I decided that I wanted to "go out" for the Sardis High School football team. Sardis was a football power, perennial county champions, so good, in fact, they usually had to play much larger schools because comparable schools were reluctant to schedule them. My father strongly objected to my decision to play football. He had reason. Not only was I small, 150 pounds and without experience, but I also had a health concern that put me at considerable risk. My father even asked the coach not to play me. But I was stubborn. The more my father objected, the more I stubbornly sought to prove him wrong! I would not get hurt. I would show him.

The season started. In the first football game I ever dressed out, I was in the starting lineup against the Altoona Choctaws, the defending 1A State Champions. Lined up against me was 6-foot-2 inch, 210-pound Bruce McAfee, who 35 years later was named by *The Gadsden Times* as the best offensive end ever to play in Etowah County. I was in way over my head!

But no one tried harder. I would prove my father wrong! By the sixth game, I was the leading receiver on the team. Then it happened — at homecoming in the second quarter, in a play where I caught a short pass, both bones were snapped in my left arm. It was over. Gene Holcomb, the head coach, who was told not to play me, came on the field; something he did twice in ten years. As they put my arm into a splint, I began to cry. It was not because of the physical pain.

As I came off the field to be taken to the hospital, I came face to face with my father. I stopped. I froze! I braced myself to hear him say the words, "I told you so!"

He never did.

ONE MINUTE MESSAGE: "For Christ came not to condemn the world, but..." John 3

Runaway Boy

Luke 15:11-32

There is a story about a young boy who was observed by one of his neighbors walking around the block time and time again, while carrying a large sack in his hand. The neighbor stopped him and said, "Well, son, I've noticed that you have been walking around the block. What's going on?"

The young boy said, "I'm running away from home."

"Oh, you are! Well, I guess that sack has your belongings in it?"

"Right."

"Let me ask you, if you are running away from home, why are you just walking around the block?"

The young boy said, "Oh, my mother told me never to cross the street."

ONE MINUTE MESSAGE: Being a part of God's family is special.

George Foreman

1 John 3:1-3

I recently saw an interview with George Foreman, twice crowned Heavyweight Champion of the World. He showed a photograph of himself and another man. He said (pointing to the other man), "That is my biological father. Even after I was Heavyweight Champion of the World, I did not know that my father was not my biological father. I found my biological father and he's a nice guy."

Then he said, "But Foreman is my father because he loved me."

ONE MINUTE MESSAGE: We can be secure in the Father's love.

Twin — Accident?

Deuteronomy 6:1-3

One of my twins asked years ago, "We were an accident, weren't we?"

"I beg your pardon!" I asked.

"We were an accident, right? I mean, our older brother was only eighteen months old when we were born. Three kids so close together. We were an accident, right?"

I exclaimed, "No! No! No! Not at all! We wanted to have our children close together. Your mother and her sister were eighteen months apart. That's what we planned for and we missed it by one day. Eighteen months and one day! If the doctor had been there on time, we'd have gotten it right on the nose. You cannot plan those kinds of things much better than that. You were anything but an accident!"

ONE MINUTE MESSAGE: No child is an accident.

Bobbie Gee

Matthew 7:7-12

Bobbie Gee tells the story of Al, a talented and gifted artist. He had two sons. The older son didn't feel well one night because of a minor stomach problem. Thinking it wasn't serious, they put him to bed. During the night, the child died from acute appendicitis. It was a horrible tragedy from which the family never recovered. The father's health began to deteriorate mentally and the mother left him with a six-year-old child. Al continued to deteriorate and became an alcoholic.

He lost it all — his home, his reputation, and his job. Years later, Al died alone in a San Francisco motel room. Bobbie Gee thought to herself about Al's wasted life but then she began to think of the younger son, Ernie, who was one of the most caring, loving, and kind people that she knew.

Bobbie Gee asked Ernie, "I know that your father raised you alone, and his life was full of many heartaches and problems. But, tell me, how did you get to be the wonderful person that you are?"

He said, "As far back as I can remember and until the day I left home at age eighteen, every night my father came into my bedroom and gave me a kiss and told me, 'Son, I love you.'"

ONE MINUTE MESSAGE: If such love could be communicated from such an imperfect parent, how much more can the love of our heavenly parent be communicated to us?

Abbie Hoffman

1 John 1:8-10

You may recall the story of Abbie Hoffman. For many years he was on the FBI's Ten Most Wanted List. He became a fugitive from the law. Hoffman was always on the run, looking over his shoulder, fearful that he would be found out or caught, waiting for the axe to fall. Then one day, after all those years, Abbie Hoffman walked into a police station and turned himself over to the authorities. "Why have you done this?" they asked.

"I'm just tired," he said. "I am just tired of running and I am tired of feeling guilty."

ONE MINUTE MESSAGE: There is a place to go with our guilt.

Hamilton's Builder

Matthew 7:24-29

J. Wallace Hamilton told the story of a wealthy builder. The wealthy builder called his top assistant, a man with whom he had a long relationship, and said, "I am going away for about ten months, and I want you to oversee the building of my house because when I return I am intending to retire… quickly."

After he left, the assistant began to think, *if the man retires, what is going to happen to me?* Besides, he has not done that much for me anyway. But he did oversee the building of the house, and at every opportunity he had, he feathered his own nest. He hired an immoral builder, hired inferior workers, and bought inferior products. He was always cutting costs and overcharging — pocketing the extra amounts.

In ten months, the builder returned and said enthusiastically; "Does it not look pretty?"

"Yes, it does," says the top assistant.

"It is beautiful!" the builder states.

"Yes, it is," the assistant agrees.

The builder then says, "Well, I got to thinking about you and I am going to retire in a couple of years… I wanted to see that you would be taken care of. The house is yours."

ONE MINUTE MESSAGE: The person you meet five years from now is the person you are becoming today.

David Livingston

Matthew 25:14-21

David Livingston stood before a group in the latter part of his ministry, his body showing the effects of many years on the mission field. With one arm hanging limp by his side, he talked for an hour to the group about the time he spent on the mission field. He told of almost starving to death, of almost dying from thirst several times, contracting diseases with high fevers, and the times he had been attacked by wild beasts.

After the talk, someone came to him and said, "Oh, Dr. Livingston, I could not help but feel sorry for you as you told about all that you did for the Lord."

He said, "Oh, please, dear Madam, if I have given you the wrong impression, I apologize. If I have left the wrong feeling with you, I apologize completely. For, you see, I was having the time of my life."

ONE MINUTE MESSAGE: The greatest joy is the adventure of following Jesus.

James Whitaker

Daniel 1:3-17

When I was in the fourth grade, I volunteered to head up a little effort to enlist boys in our class to be members of Mrs. Thomas' fourth grade basketball team. I circulated a list and people came by and signed up. The last person to sign on that list was an individual that sat in the back of the class and never said anything to anyone at any time. He was the very last one to write his name, it was written with a pencil that had not been sharpened and was almost impossible to read. I did not even turn his name into Mrs. Thomas. We had our first practice and he was there. His name was James Whitaker. At the end of the season, we were the undefeated city champions because of James Whitaker.

In 1964, at the state tournament, listed among the top five basketball players in the state of Alabama was James Whitaker. Not bad for a forward who stood only five-feet-ten and could barely write his name.

ONE MINUTE MESSAGE: I did not know he would become "that" James Whitaker.

Jennifer Jones

Romans 16:1-16

Jennifer Jones won an Academy Award for the title role in the movie, *The Song of Bernadette*. Bernadette had received a vision of the Immaculate Conception and had become quite a celebrity. An older nun was consumed by envy toward young Bernadette. In vaguely subdued anger, the nun prayed to God, "Why her? No one has prayed harder, worked longer, or suffered greater than I. Why *her* and not *me*?"

Later in the film, Bernadette collapsed while scrubbing the floor. After his examination, the doctor talked to the older nun. "Has she ever complained?"

"No, she just quietly does her work."

The doctor continued, "That's amazing… The affliction she has, she has had for a very long time. The pain is unbearable."

Later, the older nun prayed to her Lord, "God, forgive me. Thank you for the opportunity of serving the one you have chosen."

ONE MINUTE MESSAGE: The greatest joy is found in service to others.

Boy And King's Flowers

Romans 8:31-39

There is a fable told of the little boy whose mother was very ill. He gathered together what few pennies he had and went to the village to buy her some flowers. She loved flowers. When he got to the village, he found that there were none for sale. He was distraught and distressed. He wanted to do something for his mother, but he was unable to do so.

On the way home, he passed by this beautiful garden. He could not believe how beautiful that garden was. There were roses everywhere in full bloom. He stopped the manager and asked, "Can I buy some of these flowers?"

The manager said, "No, you cannot. These flowers belong to the king. They are not for sale."

With that, the little boy walked off crying. His last hope was gone when a voice was heard behind him. It was the prince, the son of the king, and he said, "You are exactly right. These flowers are not for sale. They belong to the king. But he does *give* them away."

With that, the little boy turned around and the prince loaded up both arms with long beautiful red roses to be given as a gift — a gift of grace for his mother.

ONE MINUTE MESSAGE: Do you know who that prince was? You know! You know!

Cactus Pete

Luke 9:57-62

Tim Hansel told the story when in 1932, a traveler, beaten down by the weather, half-starving, thirsting to death in the desert, wandered upon an old well. Attached to the well was a note that read, "This well has never run dry. There is water for all. Only, the leather washer gets dried out and the pump needs to be primed. West from the well you will find a rock and under the rock you will find a bottle of water corked. Take one half of the water, pour it down the well, moisten the washer and then pour the rest down the well. Pump like crazy, and you will have all the water you need. Do not drink the water that's in the bottle. Pour it all down the well. Have faith. Your friend, Cactus Pete."

ONE MINUTE MESSAGE: Are you willing to risk all to follow him?

Bishop Tutu

1 Thessalonians 5:12-15

He was a five-year-old black boy in South Africa in the days of apartheid. Those were the days of racial hatred, bigotry, and prejudice. One day, he was walking down the street on the sidewalk with his mother. In the days of apartheid, if a black person was walking down the street and they were met by a white person coming from the opposite direction on the sidewalk, they were to step out into the street and allow the white person to walk on the sidewalk. Only this time, when the white person approached that young black boy only five years old, he looked down to him and said, "Well, how are you young man? I hope you are having a good day." As he was speaking, the white man stepped out into the street and allowed the little boy and his mother to walk down the sidewalk.

As he walked past the man, the little boy looked to his mother and said, "Mama, who is that?

She said, "That is the bishop of the church."

The little boy said, "I want to be a Bishop, too." It was in the heart of that five-year-old little boy that the desire to be a Bishop was born and he became Bishop Desmond Tutu.

ONE MINUTE MESSAGE: A small act of kindness can change a life.

Bandinelli

Luke 22:1-6

His name was Pietro Bandinelli, a young man whose face was alive and full of life and vibrancy. Da Vinci chose that young man and painted his face as the face of Jesus. He found the other apostles, but the one that he had the most difficulty finding was Judas. How do you find the face that portrays that kind of misguided zeal, bigotry, and betrayal of another?

He searched for a long time and finally traveled the back alleys of the cities and there he found the man. It was a man who was a beggar, a thief, a murderer, a man who had thrown away everything decent he had ever known in all of his life. He hired him to come and be painted. The man came and sat in Da Vinci's study for several sittings and then when he went to pay him, he asked for his name and the man said, "Why Master, don't you remember me? I am Pietro Bandinelli, the man who served as the face of Jesus."

ONE MINUTE MESSAGE: Once an opportunity is lost, it is lost.

Wounded Healer

1 Peter 2:22-25

It was Henry Nouwen who quoted the great Jewish tale. He told of Joshua Ben Levi, who met the prophet Elijah and said, "Where is the Messiah? Is the Messiah here?"

Elijah said, "Why don't you ask him?"

"Go ask him? Where is he?"

Elijah said, "The Messiah is sitting at the gates of the city."

"How will I know him?" he asked.

"You will find him," Elijah responded, "sitting among the poor covered with wounds."

"How will I know the Messiah among the others who are wounded?"

"It is simple. All the others unbind all their wounds at the same time and then bind up all their wounds afterward, the Messiah is different. The Messiah unbinds the wounds one at a time and then rebinds it with the attitude: 'Perhaps I will be needed so I unbind only one at a time so I can respond as quickly as possible.'"

ONE MINUTE MESSAGE: There is no greater healer than a wounded one.

One Vote

Acts 4:36-37

In 1824, the United States was undecided about its next president. In the election, neither John Quincy Adams nor Andrew Jackson received a majority vote. The outcome of the election was tossed into the House of Representatives. The states were also equally divided. It finally came down not only to one state, the state of New York, but to *one* delegate. *One single delegate*! He was asked by Henry Clay to vote for John Quincy Adams, but he replied, "I don't like the man, but I will tell you what I will do. I will pray about it and seek God's will in the matter."

That one single delegate from New York went to bed that night and prayed until he found God's answer. Through prayer, he helped to elect the next president of the United States and also helped to determine the direction of our country.

ONE MINUTE MESSAGE: Never underestimate the power of one.

Karl Valentine

1 John 1:7-11

John Claypool told the story of Karl Valentine, who back in the 1930s, was one of the metaphysical clowns of Europe. He was sort of like some of the clown figures of our day. He dressed like a clown and acted like a clown, but yet he illustrated eternal truth. On a stage in Munich, Germany, in 1931, he went to the stage dressed as a clown. All there was upon a darkened stage was a circle of white light. The clown was down on his hands and knees and was searching for something in the lighted circle. A policeman walked by and asked him, "Sir, what are you doing?"

He replied, "I'm searching for my house keys. I have lost my house keys and I cannot get into my house without them."

With that, the policeman began helping the clown look for his keys within the circle of light. Finally, the exasperated policeman said, "Are you sure you lost the keys here?"

The clown said, "No, I lost the keys over there (pointing to a dark place on the stage)."

The policeman asked him, "If you lost the keys over there, why are you looking over here?"

And he said, "Because there is no light over there."

ONE MINUTE MESSAGE: It may be in the darkness that we find life's greatest treasures.

Umbrella

Hebrews 11:1-39

The crops were wilted. The small village had been without rain for a long period of time. This was an agricultural community that was about to lose their livelihood. The elders, the spiritual leaders of the community, said, "As a village, we're going to gather on the town square this coming Lord's Day and devote an entire hour of prayer for rain."

The people came. They brought objects of their faith. Some brought holy books, some brought rosaries, some brought crosses, and some brought other objects of their faith. As they gathered around and prayed in earnest for a solid hour, it was as if by magic the heavens opened and soft drops of rain began falling. Then they learned the greatest lesson from a nine-year-old girl who walked among the crowd. She was the only one who brought an umbrella.

ONE MINUTE MESSAGE: Faith is believing not that God can do something, but that he *will*.

Carter On Knees

Matthew 20:20-28

Habitat for Humanity is such a marvelous organization in that has done so much good throughout the world. It was told that recently a house was to be completed. The next day, it was not quite completed. During the night the project manager saw a light in the house and heard someone in the house at two o'clock in the morning. He walked into the house and there was one of the workers on his hands and knees in the kitchen, laying tile at two in the morning. "What are you doing?"

He said, "Well, the family is to move in tomorrow. I do not want them disappointed. They need to have this house completed. It needs to be complete, warm, and welcoming."

The man upon his hands and knees at two o'clock in the morning, laying kitchen tile was the former president of the United States, Jimmy Carter.

ONE MINUTE MESSAGE: The greatest of all is servant of all.

John Boyle

1 Peter 3:13-22

John Boyle was one of my professors at Southern Baptist Theological Seminary. He also taught Clinical Pastoral Education at the nearby Central State Mental Hospital in Anchorage. On one particular occasion, one of his CPE students was about to conduct his first worship service at the hospital chapel. He was very nervous. As he ascended to the pulpit, his already faulty concentration was shattered as one of the mental patients rose and began shouting, “Go to hell! Go to hell!”

The young preacher was speechless. He stood, red-faced, taken aback, while no words proceeded from his mouth.

It was then that another mental patient broke the silence when she also stood and said, “He did! He came here!”

ONE MINUTE MESSAGE: There are no limits to God’s love.

God Loves Stories

1 Samuel 1:1-28

Elie Wiesel related this story. When the great Rabbi Israel Shem Tov saw misfortune threatening the Jews, it was his custom to go into a certain part of the forest to meditate. There he would light a fire, say a special prayer, and the miracle would be accomplished and the misfortune averted.

Later, when his disciple, the celebrated Magid of Mezrith, had occasion for the same reason to intercede with heaven, he would go to the same place in the forest and say: "Master of the universe, listen! I do not know how to light the fire, but I am still able to say the prayer," and again the miracle would be accomplished.

Still later, Rabbi Mashe-leib of Sasov, in order to save his people once more, would go into the forest and say, "I do not know how to light the fire. I do not know the prayer, but I know the place and this must be sufficient." It was sufficient and the miracle was accomplished.

Then it fell to Rabbi Israel of Rizhyn to overcome misfortune. Sitting in his armchair, his head in his hands, he spoke to God, "I am unable to light the fire, and I do not know the prayer, and I cannot even find the place in the forest. All I can do is to tell the story, and this must be sufficient."

And it was sufficient. God made man because he loves stories.

ONE MINUTE MESSAGE: You are a dream, a story, in the mind of God.

Christopher Nolan

John 21:24-25

Recently, Christopher Nolan was given the prestigious British Whitbread Award for his autobiographical "novel," *Under the Eye of the Clock.* There is nothing spectacular about this latest recognition for this author/poet until you remember that he was born with severe brain damage and from infancy could only communicate with his eyes. The only way he can type is by means of a pen-like stick attached to his forehead. Each page takes twelve hours of slow, concentrated hard work. But what accounts for the triumph?

At three years of age, he said he faced the only spark within himself. He knew he was alive, wanted, and loved.

ONE MINUTE MESSAGE: The love of one can make the life of another.

Forest Carter

Revelation 7:9-17

Fred Craddock told the Forest Carter story set in the rural south during the Depression. A father was walking along the side of the house that was more like shack. He heard his two daughters on the back porch; they were laughing loudly, shrieking with joy and glee. He decided to investigate. On the old back porch, on the old wooden steps are his two daughters looking through a Sears Roebuck catalog. In that, they saw all of the beautiful clothes, all the bright colors, all the beautiful garments. They were laughing. The father came up to the children and jerked the book away from them. "Don't you ever let me see you with this book again."

He struck them just a little bit on the leg, and they ran into the house trying to stifle their sobs. The father then sat down on the back porch, buried his head in his hands, and cried like a baby.

ONE MINUTE MESSAGE: With God, we must never limit the future.

Water To Hospital

Philippians 3:7-10

A fairly recent United Press release in a midwestern city told that hospital officials had discovered that the hospital's firefighting equipment had never been connected. For 35 years, they had depended upon the equipment for the safety of their patients in case of emergency, only to find that the equipment had never been attached to the city's water main. A water pipe had extended four feet from the building and simply stopped.

ONE MINUTE MESSAGE: There is an unlimited source of power available to all… if we are connected.

Herman And Wife

Revelation 21:1-8

Chattanooga has had no finer or more eloquent preacher than Herman Battle, who for over forty years served the First Baptist Church on Eighth Street, an African American congregation. Dr. Battle was a cherished friend whose prayers brought one to the very foot of the cross. In our community-wide Good Friday service, I heard him relate the story of the home-going of his beloved wife. For 34 years they shared as close a relationship as any two people could. He was at her side for weeks during the last stages of her illness. As time drew near and she was about to meet her Lord, she turned to her husband and said, "Oh Herman, do you see them?"

"No, honey, I don't! See what? I don't see them."

"Oh Herman, don't you see them? Don't you see the lights?"

"No, honey, I don't. I don't see the lights. I wish I could, but I don't see the lights!"

Then mustering all the energy she could, she said, "You will!"

ONE MINUTE MESSAGE: God welcomes all his children home.

Carter And Missionaries

1 Thessalonians 4:1-7

President Jimmy Carter shared the story of Jermone and Joann Etheridge, Baptist missionaries to Togo. In 1976, the Etheridges felt God's calling to become missionaries. Peanut farmers, they left the security of their Plains, Georgia, home, studied French, and went to serve, teaching language and sharing tracts. Not being eloquent of speech, after several years they felt their talents could be used in better ways. They then requested and received a transfer to Moratan in northeast Togo, a region of about eighty square miles. In this area, there were only five religious entities, two Muslim and three Roman Catholic.

The missionary couple immediately began to address one of the most pressing needs of the region: good drinking water. They asked for and received from North Carolina Baptists a well-drilling machine. They dug 167 wells, 130 of which were good enough to require a pump. Now every village had good water and they were almost completely free of disease caused by the guinea worm. The missionaries then asked for and received from North Carolina Baptists a bulldozer. With this, they dug 21 ponds that caught rainfall to provide irrigation for their crops.

They also noted that the area was divided for three months every year due to the flooding of the Mono River. This peanut farmer, although certainly no engineer, with help from the locals, built a 230-foot bridge across the Mono River.

When the President visited his friends in Togo, he found within that eighty miles, 81 new churches had been built, accumulating over 5,000 new professing Christians. All because of two peanut farmers who wanted to fulfill God's calling in their lives.

ONE MINUTE MESSAGE: We all love a story. It is even better to see one.

Doris Jones

Galatians 3:26-29

Doris Jones was an elementary school teacher and a member of the church I served in Huntsville, Alabama. With laughter in her voice, she related to me an experience that she had. After a long summer, she was talking with one of her best friends with whom she had taught for years. "I want you to meet my son," her friend stated. "This is his first day of school. Oh, there he is — over there with those other boys at the bicycle rack."

"Which one?" Doris questioned.

Her African-American friend responded, "Well, Doris! There are five white boys over there and one black boy. Which one do you think is mine?"

Doris laughed more heartily in telling me the story. "I just saw children."

ONE MINUTE MESSAGE: God is color-blind.

Buck And Curtain

Matthew 16:24-28

Fred Craddock told the following story: I used to go home to west Tennessee, where an old high school chum of mine had a restaurant. I called him Buck. I'd go home for Christmas and say, "Merry Christmas, Buck," and I'd get a piece of chess pie and cup of coffee, free.

One year I went in, "Merry Christmas, Buck." He said, "Let's go for coffee."

I said, "What's the matter? Isn't this the restaurant?"

He said, "I don't know, sometimes I wonder."

We went for coffee. We sat there and pretty soon he said, "Did you see the curtain?"

I said, "Buck, I saw the curtain. I always see the curtain."

What he meant by curtain is this: They have a number of buildings in that little town; they're called shotgun buildings. They're long buildings and have two entrances, front and back. One's off the street, and one's off the alley, with a curtain and the kitchen in the middle. If you're white, you come in off the street; if you're black, you come in off the alley. He said, "Did you see the curtain?"

I said, "I saw the curtain."

He said, "The curtain has to come down."

I said, "Good. Bring it down."

He said, "That's easy for you to say. Come in here from out of state and tell me how to run my business."

I said, "Okay, leave it up."

He said, "I can't leave it up."

I said, "Well, then take it down."

"I can't take it down." He was in terrible shape. After a while he said, "If I take that curtain down, I lose a lot of my customers. If I leave that curtain up, I lose my soul."

ONE MINUTE MESSAGE: If one gains the world, and loses his soul…

Phil Donahue

Ephesians 2:1-10

When television personality Phil Donohue first came into prominence, it was from a television station in Cincinnati, Ohio. Since I lived in southern Indiana, I often caught the show. On one particular episode, he was interviewing representatives from a group called "Freedom From Religion." Oh, how they complained! They bemoaned all the atrocities created in the name of religion down through the ages. Embarrassingly, the list was not a short one. They complained about how they were forced to be subjected to religious views not their own, some even in the market place.

Then a caller phoned in and remarked, "You are right. The church has made many mistakes and often is wrong. But I am sure that you are aware that the church has founded dozens of orphanages, hundreds of schools, countless hospitals, fed millions, and has sent thousands of missionaries to give medical and agricultural assistance to un-churched people in need."

The caller went on and on in an unlimited litany of good that had been accomplished. She then stated, "Now, what have you folks ever done besides belly ache?"

The Freedom From Religion group was dumbfounded. They even got into a huddle of discussion only to emerge with the remark, "We are working on that!"

Sure they are.

ONE MINUTE MESSAGE: It is much easier to complain than to do something about our being disgruntled.

Richard Foster

Luke 18:1-8

Richard Foster, the great Quaker author, was in our congregation last year. He was asked the question, "How do you become a writer?"

His answer was ingenius. He said that first you must go to your favorite department store: Wal-Mart, K-Mart, or whatever. There, you buy the largest container of glue that they sell. A gallon would suffice. You then take the gallon of glue home, enter your study, pour the glue into your desk chair, and then place your rear end in the glue. The best way to become a writer is to stick to it. Pardon the pun!

ONE MINUTE MESSAGE: Success is often one percent inspiration and 99% perspiration.

Put World Together

Ephesians 2:11-22

John Claypool told the story of the father babysitting his rambunctious young son. The father was dead set on reading his newspaper, only to be continually interrupted by his active offspring demanding his attention. The boy kept asking questions, playing the television too loud, wanting to play games, all in an effort to disturb this occupied parent. It was then that the father noticed a map of the world on the back page of the paper. He took a pair of scissors, cut the map into pieces, and handed them to his son with the instructions to put the map together. *That will occupy him for a while*, he thought. Wrong! In an amazingly short period of time the young lad presented to his father the map completely assembled.

"Wow! That is unbelievable. How did you put the map together so quickly?" the father asked.

"It was easy, Daddy. There was a picture of a man on the other side. You put the man together. You put the world together."

ONE MINUTE MESSAGE: The meaning of the universe is found in the sacrificial death of Jesus.

Rogers On Camera

Colossians 1:15-27

Did you see the first episode of the new "Candid Camera" in 1998? Guests were ushered into a very expensive hotel room and then told that the television did not work. The hidden camera recorded their responses of anger, frustration, and disgruntlement. The fourth guest was a recognizable surprise, Fred Rogers. Yes, that Mr. Rogers who was somewhat out of his neighborhood. He, too, had the news sprung upon him that the television did not work. He very graciously responded, "Oh that's okay; I will be all right!"

"But you don't understand, it won't work!" the man prodded.

Again, Mr. Rogers answered kindly, "I would not have used it anyway. It's all right."

The "hotel employee" then literally did everything he could to provoke his famous guest, only to have Fred respond every time with kindness, gentleness, and patience.

ONE MINUTE MESSAGE: It is so good to see on the outside what you perceive someone to be on the inside.

Are You Jesus?

John 15:1-17

I first read this story in the writings of Keith Miller over thirty years ago. It remains a classic. It seemed that a businessman had resolved in his heart to act like a Christian instead of just talking like one. His high resolve was put to the test as he was hurrying through a crowded airport, luggage in hand, trying to catch the plane for which he was already woefully late. Running hard, watching his watch, he failed to see a small boy crossing his path with an arm load full of puzzles. He accidentally side-swiped the lad, sending puzzle pieces everywhere. The businessman clutched his luggage and began to set out again in his quest to catch his plane.

Then he looked into the eyes of the little boy and he could go no further. He set his luggage down, got down on his knee, and began to help the lad pick up the pieces as his plane left without him. During the several minutes they worked together the lad said not a word. As he accepted them, the boy looked up to the man, with the moisture of a tear in his eye, and said, "Mister, are you Jesus?"

And, you know, for a minute there, he was!

ONE MINUTE MESSAGE: Jesus is all around for those who wish to see.

Baloney

Galatians 6:7-10

It was many years ago now, right after I had first started in the ministry, that Sharlon and I traveled to Little River Canyon in Fort Payne, Alabama. Somehow along the trail we were separated and I found myself alone standing on the rim of the canyon, viewing a vast expanse of indescribable beauty. Looking across to the other side, I shouted at the top of my voice, "Baloney!"

Nothing came back. This is my chance, I thought to myself. Seeing that there was no one else around, I shouted as loudly as I could, "I'm the greatest preacher in all the world!"

And the voice came back, "Baloney!"

Some might say it is the law of the echo, "You get back in return what you send out."

ONE MINUTE MESSAGE: You get what you give.

Harrington O 'Hair

Hebrews 6:13-20

Many remember that before Phil Donohue gained national, even worldwide fame, he began as a talk-show host in a local station in Cincinnati. Living in Indiana at the time, I remember when he hosted his then soon-to-be famous debates between evangelist Bob Harrington, the "Chaplain of Bourbon Street" and the infamous atheist and political activist, Madelyn Murray O'Hair. The one I remember seeing was a doozy! Ms. O'Hair would rant and rave on endlessly about the general abuses of religion and Christians in particular. She would posited her confident position that the Bible was full of fairy tales and the stance of faith was folly from any point of human reason. Reverend Harrington patiently waded through her diatribe and then responded succinctly to her with his own views and then remarked, "I believe it because I want to."

ONE MINUTE MESSAGE: If life is to have meaning, we must choose to hope.

Monterrey Dream

Hebrews 11:1-7

I began playing Little League baseball in 1957. The story that year in baseball circles was about a small band of diminutive Little Leaguers from Monterrey, Mexico. They walked across the American border, some wearing shoes for the first time. They were huge underdogs in every game they played. But they won. Against all odds, they won and won.

In the Little League finals at Williamsport, the Monterrey street kids played the highly favored California team, which outweighed the Mexicans thirty pounds per person. Led by the switch-pitching Angel Macias, the lads from across the border not only shocked the world by upsetting the California bunch, but Macias pitched a no-hitter, striking out eleven in six innings.

Monterrey won the world championship. A film about the team was called *How Tall Is a Giant?* The story ended with an answer to the question—as tall as courage, as tall as faith, as tall as a dream.

ONE MINUTE MESSAGE: Hope is built upon dreams.

Sorry Not Sorry

Hosea 5:8-15

John Claypool first told me the story of the old sailor very apparently lying upon his death bed. Some who cared for him summoned the priest, a young novice with little experience in such eternal matters. The young man began his nervous remarks by saying, "I am sure, sir, that you are aware of your serious condition and undoubtedly wish to make amends and express regret for your sins."

The "old salt" thought for a moment and then responded, "Well, Father, to be honest with you, I am not sorry for the life I have lived. I have enjoyed my life of wine, women, and song, and do not wish to leave this world with a lie upon my lips."

The young priest was taken aback. He hardly knew how to respond, and then a moment of true inspiration arrived as he said, "Then tell me, sir. Can you truly say that you are sorry that you are not sorry?"

A mist began to appear in the eyes of the old sailor. "Yes, Padre, I can truly say that, I'm sorry that I am not sorry."

ONE MINUTE MESSAGE: It only takes a small crack to open the door to repentance.

My Brother Paul

Mark 3:31-35

The great storyteller Father William Bausch first related to me the following true story. It seemed that a small village had located itself around the seacoast lighthouse and dedicated itself to the rescue efforts necessary when the storms raged upon the sea. On this particular occasion, the storm was particularly violent. It seemed to spend its fury endlessly. It was known that a ship was in jeopardy. Rescue teams were sent out. They returned and were sent out again. Some workers returned; a few did not.

The last of the teams came back, exhausted and spent, with the news that there was at least one more survivor, one more to save. A young man raised his hand and volunteered to lead a team back upon the stormy sea to rescue the lone survivor. His mother protested. "You cannot go… You are too young. I have already lost your brother, Paul. I cannot lose you."

"But I must go," he said. "It is what I should do."

"You cannot," his mother cried clinging to him.

"I have to," he replied. And with that, he broke away from his mother to lead the life-saving efforts.

They were gone and gone. Hours crept past. Fires were lit upon the coast as beacons. Some went to pray. Others paced furiously and worried nervously. After what seemed to be an eternity, word was heard. A message was sent from the young man. "Tell Mama I'm okay. Tell Mama we found the survivor. Tell Mama, it's my brother, Paul."

ONE MINUTE MESSAGE: Sometimes we have to do what we have to do.

Reginald Denny

Matthew 18:21-35

You saw it on television. I saw it on television. I was horrified. From a helicopter view during the Los Angeles riots, two men dragged a truck driver from the cab of his truck and beat him over the head with a broken bottle and kicked his face until it was totally disfigured. A short time later, Reginald Denny, the man who was beaten so severely, was in court against the people who had beaten him. His face was still swollen and misshapen. He was sitting in court with the defendants who had committed that horrible crime. They were all sitting there, sullen, hostile, no yielding whatsoever. Against the protest of his lawyers, Reginald Denny went across the courtroom to the mothers of those defendants, hugged them, and told them that he forgave their sons. One mother looked into his eyes and said, "I love you."

ONE MINUTE MESSAGE: Someone has to break the cycle of hatred and revenge — and God has.

Bob Crawford

John 11:45-57

Bob Crawford was one of the finest Christians it has ever been my privilege to serve as pastor. Struck down by cancer in his forties, this courageous Christian exemplified unbelievable courage as he combated this dreaded disease and lived longer with his particular cancer than anyone in recorded medical history. Bob's courage taught us how to live and taught us how to die. It began early in his life.

After his funeral service, a lady came up to me and said, "My name is Regina Ward and I knew Bob in high school. In 1966, Bob and were classmates at Rossville High School. There were 2,500 students there and I became 2,500 and one. I integrated Rossville High School in 1966." She said, "There were students there who called me names. There were students who shoved and pushed me, and there were students who shot spit wads at me. Bob Crawford, even then as a teenager, stood between me and them, shielding me from those taunts and jeers, and those who pushed and shoved, and those who hit me with spit wads."

Bob Crawford lived the last years of his life with one foot in one world and one foot in another.

ONE MINUTE MESSAGE: It sometimes is unpopular to stand up for what is right.

Kind Folks Live Here?

Matthew 4:18-22

Years ago, in the days of horse and buggy, an old man would sit and whittle on the front porch of his house that sat at the entrance to the small village in which he lived. He served as an unofficial greeter to any and all who might happen to pass by. On one such occasion, he was approached by a wagon-load of travelers who inquired, "Pardon us, sir, but what kind of folks live here?"

The old man hit a lick or two with his knife on the whittling stick and asked, "Well, what kind of folks did you find in the place from which you came?"

"Wonderful people! Kind and friendly. May be the best people we've ever known. We hated to leave."

"Well, I guess that's the kind of folks you are going to find here."

Several hours later another wagon load approached the front porch sitter. "Pardon us, sir but what kind of folks live here?"

"Well, what kind of folks did you find in the place from which you came?"

They replied, "Mean and spiteful! We couldn't wait to leave."

Then the old man said, "Well, I guess that's the kind of folks you are going to find here."

ONE MINUTE MESSAGE: We usually find what we are looking for.

Squash

Galatians 6:7-10

When I was fifteen years old, we moved from the city to an eight-acre "farm" in the country with a barn, pigs, cattle, and everything. My father immediately wanted to plant a garden like he did as a boy when he lived on a farm. We had a wonderful place in which to do so between the house and the barn, all fenced and laid out in 100-feet rows. The problem was, however, that it had been a few harvests since anyone in our clan had sowed a garden. So, we went to the feed store and bought seeds of every sample: beans, corn, squash, a literal cornucopia! My mother loved squash. So, we planted squash. We planted a 100-feet row of squash. Now, if you know anything about planting a garden, you know that three or four hills of squash will feed Cox's Army. We had 100 feet!

We then wanted to plant butter beans. But we could not find the butter beans. We surmised that we must have planted the butter beans instead of the squash. So, we planted another 100-feet of squash!

We had 200-feet of squash. We grew tons of squash! No one in our family even liked squash except my mother! We gave it away, threw it away, threw it at each other — we had tons of squash. Oh yes, a few weeks later we found that in the corner of the fence, we had many butter bean vines growing where we had misplaced and spilled them.

Was God punishing us because of our carelessness and stupidity by causing so much squash to grow? No! I think, I am not sure about this, but I think that we grew squash because we planted squash. That does seem reasonable, doesn't it?

ONE MINUTE MESSAGE: Vance Havner said, “Many folks sow their wild oats all week long and come to church on Sunday to pray for crop failure.”

Ford #1

Luke 11:5-8

Dan grew up as I did in the baseball-crazy town of Gadsden, Alabama, in the 1950s. Two years my junior, Dan was a good baseball player. Dan was a great football player. But Dan's fondest ambition was to be a coach. So, while still a high school student, Dan coached the Coosa Federal Little League baseball team. In his very first season, Dan's team had a perfect record. The played eighteen games and they lost eighteen games. But they would not quit, and in his second season, Dan's record improved 100%. They won one game. They played eighteen games and lost *only* seventeen. Dan's coaching record at the end of two years was one win and 35 losses.

Needless to say, no one was asking Dan to lead a coaching clinic or address a civic club. But Dan did not lose heart. He loved his kids. He often took them to church, especially if a Christian athlete was speaking. He taught them to persevere.

In 1981, Dan's team had another perfect record, only it was not baseball but football. And Dan's team, the Clemson Tigers, had a perfect record of 13 and 0 and were crowned NCAA National Football Champions. And Dan, Danny Ford, was chosen NCAA National Coach of the Year, the youngest ever so chosen.

ONE MINUTE MESSAGE: Never quit!

Ford #2

Philippians 4:8-10

In the mid 1990s, Danny was no longer the coach of the Clemson Tigers, but was head football coach of the Arkansas Razorbacks. Danny was taking his "Hogs" into Tuscaloosa to do battle with the University of Alabama Crimson Tide, his alma mater. No coach ever wanted to win a game more than Coach Ford.

The game began and from the outset it was nip and tuck. Tight and tense, it was a game where any one play could decide the outcome. Deep in the fourth quarter, the atmosphere was electric — then came one of the most crucial plays of the game. The Arkansas quarterback threw a pass in the flat to the Razorback tight end. He was wide open. There was not an Alabama defender to be seen. The Arkansas player could have run all day and probably scored the deciding touchdown. But he dropped the ball! Wide open, and he dropped the ball! He not only dropped the ball before the television audience, before 80,000 fans in Bryant-Denny Stadium, he dropped the ball right in front of the Arkansas bench, and yes, right in front of the Arkansas head football coach, Danny Ford. The player just stood there. You could tell that he wanted to cry. He wished that the earth would open up and swallow him whole. He just stood there with anguish painted on his face.

It was then that Danny Ford ran out onto the field, ran right up to the embarrassed player, got right up in his face, opened wide his arms, and hugged the tight end as tightly as he could. Even the announcers remarked, "What parent would not want his (her) child to play for Danny Ford?"

ONE MINUTE MESSAGE: The best thing about making right choices is the kind of person you become.

Newspaper Boy

Colossians 1:1-14

A Sunday school teacher had noticed a young boy delivering newspapers on Sunday morning during the Sunday school hour. He began to pray for that boy. He then began to feel that God wanted him to do more. The next Sunday, he saw the lad again. The Sunday school teacher approached him and invited him in, but got the stern reply, "Do you see this stack of papers, mister? If I don't sell them, I don't eat. My mother is sick in bed, my dad's dead, and this is our living."

The Sunday school teacher then taught his finest lesson, as he went with the young man to deliver every paper! That young man is now one of the leading surgeons of that state and the chairman of deacons of that church.

ONE MINUTE MESSAGE: Praying for others can help us to become a part of the answer to our prayer.

City Everywhere

Philippians 1:3-11

The story was titled "The City of Everywhere" and was written by Hugh Price Hughes. It was a story of a traveler who went by train to a city where he had never been. When he got off the train, he noticed that everyone there was just like the people in all of the other places he had been except for one thing. No one was wearing shoes! "Odd," he thought.

He commented to the first person he met in the train station about no one wearing shoes. The man said, "That's right."

The traveler said, "No one is wearing shoes, are they?"

"That is true."

The traveler said, "Let me ask you another question. Why aren't you wearing shoes? Do you not believe in shoes?"

"Oh yes," the man said, "I believe in shoes."

"Well, then why aren't you wearing shoes?"

"Ah, why aren't we wearing shoes? That's the question."

He went into a restaurant, same scene, no one was wearing shoes. He asked another individual, "Sir, may I ask you a question? I notice that you are not wearing shoes. Are shoes not available to you? Do you not believe in shoes?"

"Oh yes, shoes are available. We believe in shoes."

"Well, why are you not wearing shoes?"

"Ah. Why aren't we wearing shoes? That is the question."

Befuddled totally, the man left the restaurant, walked down the street, and stopped the first man he saw. "Sir, I notice you are not wearing shoes. I understand you know about shoes, and I understand that shoes are fully available to you. Do you not know the benefits of wearing shoes?"

The man said, "Of course, we know the benefits of wearing shoes. Go down that street and you will see the finest shoe factory in this part of the country. Every week the manager of the shoe factory talks to us about the benefits of wearing shoes."

The traveler said, "Let me get this straight. You know about shoes, you believe in shoes, you know the benefits of wearing shoes, and shoes are available to you. Then, pray tell me, why aren't you wearing shoes?"

"Why aren't we wearing shoes? Ah, that is the question."

ONE MINUTE MESSAGE: Why don't we pray?

Big Rocks

Ephesians 2:11-22

In seeking to create that teachable moment, the motivational speaker presented to his gathered students a large, clear, empty glass container. He filled it with several large rocks, after which he asked his eager onlookers, "Is this container full?" Almost no one responded in the affirmative. As if to agree with them, he then placed within the contained several smaller rocks which filled some of the spaces left by the larger ones. "Is this now full?" About one half responded in the affirmative. The teacher then took a pail of sand, and poured it into the container, filling the small spaces left by the smaller rocks. "Is this full now?" Whereupon the mentor then took a pitcher of water and poured almost all of its contents into the container. Now the container was full.

Then he posed to his attentive audience the question, "Now, what have you learned? What is the point of the demonstration?"

The consensus seemed to be that the revealed truth was, "You can always put in more stuff!"

To which the insistent instructor responded, "No! The most important lesson to be learned is — you put the big rocks in first."

ONE MINUTE MESSAGE: The main thing is to keep the main thing the *main thing*.

Wait So Long

Revelation 3:19-22

William Bausch reminded us of a very famous picture that you have probably seen reproduced many times: The picture of Jesus standing outside a door overgrown with ivy. There's no knocker, no handle on the outside. The idea is that Jesus stands there and knocks, but there's no way for him to enter unless someone on the other side of the door decides to open it and let him in. It's called *The Light of the World* and it's in Saint Paul's Cathedral in London.

Those of you who have been to London know that Saint Paul's has, for a long time, been situated in a very busy, commercialized area with heavy traffic. The result is that the picture got quite dirty and the cathedral staff sent it to one of those places that restores art pieces. But when the restorers took the picture out of its frame to clean it, they saw something no one was intended to see. On the bottom, underneath the molding, the artist had written the words, "Forgive me, Lord Jesus, that I kept you waiting so long!"

Well…?

ONE MINUTE MESSAGE: Why are we waiting?

Someone Like That

Luke 6:37

It is a true story. He was a soldier who distinguished himself at West Point. He was sent to Vietnam and distinguished himself there with bravery and courage. A group of men under his leadership met enemy fire. In fact, they were trapped, but because of his courage and determination he was able to lead every member of his group from the enemy fire, except one who was severely wounded. All night long the young lieutenant heard the cry of the wounded man. He could stand it no longer. So he crossed the zone of crossfire, picked up the wounded man, and took him back to the foxhole. Just as the young lieutenant was about to step in himself, a bullet caught him in the back and he was killed instantly. He saved the man's life at the expense of his own.

His parents were crushed. Months later, they heard that the young man whose life their son had saved was in town. They invited him to their home for dinner just to meet him. The young man accepted, but it was a disaster. The man was obnoxious and rude. He was drunk, told off-color stories, and did everything in his power to insult the graciousness of the home that was extended to him. The evening was a nightmare. Finally, the belligerent and hostile man left. They slammed the door and the mother fell on her knees in tears and said, "Just think, our precious son died for somebody like that."

Yes ma'am, He did!

ONE MINUTE MESSAGE: God is gracious to the ungrateful and the wicked.

Lithograph Picasso

Matthew 6:6

In July, 1975, the “Nashville Banner” ran an article about David Burroughs. David Burroughs was an art collector who just happened to stop by a garage sale. When he saw what he saw, he could not believe his eyes. There was an individual who was selling all of her possessions to join a commune. One of the possessions she was selling was a black and white lithograph that he purchased for $5.00. He thought that he knew what it was, but when he got home, he found his appraisal to be authentic. It was in fact an original Picasso. For $5.00, she had sold a painting that was worth thousands and thousands of dollars for the cheap thrill, if you will, of joining a commune.

She had it, but she just did not get it.

ONE MINUTE MESSAGE: Don’t squander the valuable gift of life.

Little Tree Turkeys

2Timothy 1:3-7

Forrest Carter wrote a wonderful book, *The Education of Little Tree,* in which he told the following story. It is the story of a young Native American boy named Little Tree. When Little Tree was left an orphan, he was sent to live with his Cherokee grandparents in the Smoky Mountains. Soon the grandfather began to teach Little Tree about the way of his people.

One day grandfather and grandson went hunting. The old man dug a hole in the ground and made a turkey trap. When they returned hours later, six turkeys were gobbling in the trap.

All six turkeys were removed from the trap and their legs securely bound. As they lay squawking and flapping on the ground, the grandfather told Little Tree that they only needed three turkeys. Then he went on to explain that they should choose the three smallest and least likely to survive and set the others free to reproduce and provide food for someone else. In this graphic way, Little Tree learned that the way of his people is to be as concerned with giving to life as much as taking from life.

These kinds of lessons in contentment will result in practical deeds of good for others. It is a way to give back, out of the gratitude we have for the abundance we have been given.

ONE MINUTE MESSAGE: What are we giving or leaving to our children or grandchildren?

Dad Was A Lot Of Fun

John 15:1-11

Bruce Larson told about a friend down in Montgomery, Alabama. A few years ago he told Bruce an unforgettable story of a summer vacation he had planned for his wife and children. He was unable to go himself because of business, but he helped them plan every day of a camping trip in the family station wagon from Montgomery all the way to California, up and down the west coast and then back to Montgomery.

He knew their route exactly and the precise time they would be crossing the Great Divide. The friend arranged to fly himself out to the nearest airport and hire a car and a driver to take him to a place which every car must pass. He sat by the side of the road for several hours, waiting for the sight of that familiar station wagon. When it came into view, he stepped out on the road and put his thumb out to hitch hike a ride with the family who assumed he was 3,000 miles away.

Bruce said to him, "Coleman, I'm surprised they didn't drive off the road in terror or drop dead of a heart attack. What an incredible story. Why did you go to all that trouble?"

"Well, Bruce," he said, "someday I'm going to be dead and when that happens, I want my kids and my wife to say, 'You know, Dad sure was a lot of fun.'"

ONE MINUTE MESSAGE: How much fun are you?

Youngdahl

1 Thessalonians 5:1-3

Rueben Youngdahl told the following story: An estate was expertly tended by a caretaker. Every tree was trimmed, the grass cut, and stately beds of flowers were in bloom. Yet not a soul was around to take in the beauty, except the caretaker. A visitor asked, "When was the owner last here?"

"Twelve years ago!"

"Then from whom do you get your instructions?"

"From his agent in Milan."

"But does he ever visit the estate to inspect it?"

"No."

"And yet you keep it trim as if he would come tomorrow?"

The gardener interrupted to say, "As if he would come today, sir. As if he would come today!"

ONE MINUTE MESSAGE: Don't put off for tomorrow what you can do today.

U. S. Grant

Matthew 25:31-46

Ulysses S. Grant fought many significant battles as commander of the Union forces in the war between the states. He also served as President of the United States, where he probably engaged in as many battles as he did while he was a general. Toward the end of his life he fought his toughest battle — with cancer and death.

It was during the last encounter that one of his former generals, O. O. Howard, came to visit the former commander-in-chief. Howard had a well-known reputation for being a religious man. As they reminisced about battles gone by, Grant stopped his friend in mid-sentence and asked, "Howard, tell me what you know about prayer."

ONE MINUTE MESSAGE: We may not have to live with the poor, but we will die with them.

Fred's Cigar

Romans 8:12-17

Fred Craddock told the story of being invited to a particular place to speak. Of all places, they made arrangements for him to stay in a nursing home. They even made arrangements for him to have his evening meals there. The director of the nursing home told him to be careful about where he sat in the dining room because the patients already had their pre-arranged places for seating.

After everyone was seated, he looked over the room and saw a man sitting by himself, so he sat with him. As he struck up a conversation with the gentleman, he asked, "What did you do?"

The man said, "I was in the Marine Corps Band and played the trumpet for 34 years."

Dr. Craddock said, "You must have had a lot of wonderful experiences."

The man replied, "Yes, I did. I played for five presidents."

Dr. Craddock said, "Well, that must have been wonderful."

"It was," the man answered. "One time when Franklin Roosevelt invited Winston Churchill over, we played for him. Afterward, Churchill mingled among us. Churchill came to me and said, 'You play a good trumpet, there. Here, have a cigar.'

I said, "No thank you, I don't smoke." A thousand times I have wished I had taken that cigar! Why didn't I take that cigar? If I had taken that cigar, I could walk over this room and show people that cigar and say, 'Winston Churchill gave me this cigar.' I would be somebody. Now, I am nobody."

ONE MINUTE MESSAGE: We are somebody because God says we are.

Norman Cousins

Ecclesiastes 3:4

The Anatomy of An Illness: As Perceived by the Patient was written by former Saturday Review editor Norman Cousins, who was hospitalized in 1964 with an extremely rare, crippling disease. When conventional medicine failed to improve his condition and he was diagnosed as incurable, Cousins checked out of the hospital. Being aware of the harmful effects that negative emotions can have on the human body, Cousins reasoned that the reverse also might be true. He decided to dwell on becoming well again.

He borrowed a movie projector and prescribed his own treatment plan, consisting of Marx Brothers motion pictures and old "Candid Camera" reruns on film. He studied all aspects of his disease and with the help of his physician learned what would have to take place in his body to make it "right" again. In his book, he recounts that he "made the joyous discovery that ten minutes of genuine belly laughter would give me at least two hours of pain-free sleep."

What had seemed to be a progressively debilitating, fatal cellular disease was reversed and, in time, Cousins completely recovered. After his personal account of his victory appeared in the "New England Journal of Medicine," he received more than 3,000 letters from appreciative physicians throughout the world. Thirty-four medical schools have included his article in their instructional materials and in 1978, Norman Cousins joined the faculty of the UCLA Medical School.

ONE MINUTE MESSAGE: Had a good laugh lately?

Faust And Satan

John 8:1-11

There's a famous painting in which the artist depicted the great interview between Faust and Satan. Faust gambled for his soul. The painting pictures the two sitting at a chessboard, the devil on one side and Faust on the other. The devil leered with delight over the checkmate of Faust's lonely king and knight.

Contemplation of the painting leaves one with the conclusion that Faust is completely beaten and at the mercy of Satan. Faust's expression is one of hopeless worry. Satan gloats with superiority. But one day, a world famous master of chess went to the gallery in London to view the picture. He spent hours meditating over the seemingly impossible situation it depicted. He paced back and forth. Then, to the utter amazement and surprise of the other art viewers in the gallery, he shouted a discovery which echoed around the marble corridors. "It's a lie!" he blurted out. "It's a lie! The king and the knight have another move!"

ONE MINUTE MESSAGE: With God, there is always another chance — and another and another….

F. D. R.

James 1:19-25

It was President Franklin D. Roosevelt who grew weary of the mindless chatter, the smooth and empty talk so characteristic of Washington in general and White House receptions in particular. He was tired of those, so full of their own intentions and objectives, who would look past everyone and would truly listen to no one. At one such reception, he would extend a firm and confident handshake, flash the huge familiar smile and say, "I murdered my grandmother this morning."

With only one exception, everyone smiled and responded with thoughtless remarks like, "Oh, how lovely!" or "You're doing a fine job!" The only exception was foreign diplomat who responded without missing a beat, "Well, I'm sure she had it coming to her!"

ONE MINUTE MESSAGE: When you truly listen to someone, you are giving to them the best gift of all — yourself!

Poor Sinner

Luke 23:39-43

The wonderful Roman Catholic storyteller, William Bausch, related: In Vienna, Austria, you will find a church in which the Hapsburgs, the former ruling family of Austria, are buried. It is said that when royal funerals finally arrive at the church for the burial rites, the mourners leading the funeral procession knock at the door to gain entrance. "Who is it that desires admission here?" a priest asks through the locked door.

"His apostolic majesty, the emperor!" calls the guard.

"I don't know him," answers the priest.

A second knock follows and a similar question is asked. This time, the funeral guard announces the deceased as the "the highest emperor."

Again, "I don't know him," echoes throughout the vaulted burial chamber. Finally a third knock is heard. "Who is it?"

"A poor sinner; your brother," comes the final answer. Then the door is opened and the royal burial completed.

ONE MINUTE MESSAGE: We are all sinners saved by the grace of God.

Whitcomb Brougher

Romans 3:21-30

J. Whitcomb Brougher was one of the finest, if not one of the most colorful, pastors in the 150-year history of Chattanooga's First Baptist Church, serving around the turn of the century, not the last one, the one before that. His book, *Life and Laughter,* is a classic. He may be best remembered, however, when he announced and then publicized that he would be preaching on the social sins of Chattanooga and that he would be naming sins and calling names!

Needless to say, the attendance for that service was overwhelming, even overflowing. The attendance was so abundant, even out in the streets, that the preacher could not get into the building. A fire truck and ladder was utilized to lift Dr. Brougher up to a window in the church and he preached from the window to the crowds gathered below.

I thought about doing that one Sunday morning, naming sins and calling names. But I was afraid that if I did, my name might head the list.

ONE MINUTE MESSAGE: Don't take yourself too seriously.

Armenian Earthquake

1 Corinthians 13:4-7

In 1989, Armenia was almost leveled by an 8.2 earthquake. The quake killed over 30,000 people in less than four seconds. A father left his wife securely at home and rushed to the school to search for his son. When he arrived at the school site, his heart was so saddened and a lump came up in his throat because the school building was flattened.

All the way there, he kept thinking of the words he had told his son dozens and dozens of times, "I will always be there for you, no matter what." As he looked at that rubble and saw hopelessness written all over it, those words came back. "I will always be there, no matter what."

He began to search his mind and remembered the room that probably housed his son. He went there and stone by stone, began uncovering the rubble. Other parents arrived and they said, "There's no use to go on. It's too late. They are all dead. It's hopeless."

But yet he continued and turned to them and asked, "Will you not help me?" but no one helped.

A few minutes later the fire chief came and said, "It's impossible. The building is still crumbling, fires are being set, and explosions are happening, get away! You're only making matters worse."

The father turned and asked, "Will you not help me?" But no one helped.

A few moments later the police came. They tried to drag him away physically but he continued. Stone by stone — he pulled this rock and that rock, remembering the words to his son, "I will be there for you, no matter what."

He dug for eight hours… twelve hours… 24 hours… 36 hours… then, in hour 38, he pulled a boulder and heard his son's voice. He screamed his son's name, "Armand!"

He heard back, "Daddy, I knew you would come! I knew you would come! I told them that if you were alive you would come."

The father asked, "Son, what's going on?"

The son replied, "Daddy, we're scared, hungry, thirsty, and thankful you're here. Fourteen of 33 are still living."

The father said, "Come to me, son."

And the boy replied,"No, Daddy, you let all of them go first because I know no matter what, you will be there for me."

ONE MINUTE MESSAGE: Love perseveres.

Astor

Matthew 13:1-9

C. Roy Angel related the story of a hotel clerk serving his time in a small third-class hotel in Philadelphia when a tired, elderly couple arrived late in the night. The man pleaded, "Can you rent us a room? We had no idea of the big conventions that were in town. We arrived late. All the hotels where we usually stay are full. It is past midnight and we are bone-weary-tired. Can you help us?"

"Well, we, too, are full. But I work at night and sleep during the day. It is not much, but you can have my room for the night." The couple accepted the offer with undying gratitude.

The next morning, the couple came down to the clerk amazingly refreshed. "You are too fine a hotel man to stay here!" the elderly man exclaimed. "Why don't you let me return to New York City, build a five-star luxurious hotel, and pay you to be the general manager?"

The clerk was dumbfounded and he even thought the man might not be properly connected with reality. He managed to say, "That sounds wonderful!"

It was then that the man introduced himself as John Jacob Astor. He did return to New York City, he did build the Waldorf Astoria, and the Philadelphia night clerk became the best-known hotel man in the world.

ONE MINUTE MESSAGE: Sometimes we reap more than we sow.

Schoolmaster

Proverbs 22:6

There is an old tale of a German schoolmaster who, every day, would go and bow down before the students in his class. He did it every single day and someone asked him, "Why are you doing this? Why is a schoolmaster bowing before his students?"

He said, "You never know! You never know who or what one of these students might become."

One of those students was a young man by the name of Martin Luther.

ONE MINUTE MESSAGE: You never know!

Alms Box

Matthew 6:19-21

There is the story of the minister who was called to be the supply preacher on Sunday at a small rural church. As he often did on such occasions, he took his small son with him. The arrangements were that he was to meet the layperson in charge of the service in the small foyer of the sanctuary. While waiting with his son, he noticed a small box in the foyer labeled, "Alms for the needy!"

He thought to himself, "Why not?" So, he reached into his wallet, took out a one-dollar bill and placed it in the box. The layperson showed up, took him into the sanctuary, and eventually introduced him. He preached his sermon and everything went well.

After the service was concluded, the same layperson explained, "We are a small church and have nothing in the budget to pay a supply preacher. We just give to him whatever is contained in the Alms box." He turned the box over and emptying into the preacher's hands was only his own one-dollar bill.

As his son and he were walking to the car, the boy remarked, "You know, Dad, if you had put more into that box, you would have gotten more out!"

ONE MINUTE MESSAGE: We usually get out of something what we put in.

Curbs On Cornfields

2 Kings 23:1-3

In the early part of the twentieth century, Henry Ford and his brother-in-law Howell Graves visited Muscle Shoals, Alabama. They announced to a nation that Muscle Shoals was to become the "Detroit of the South." Henry Ford was going to build automobile making facilities in Muscle Shoals to rival those of the north. The city would become, in one word, "prosperous." Henry Ford laid out an entire city, complete with subdivisions. He paved roads, put down sidewalks, laid sewer lines, and curbed and guttered an entire section of the city which once had been corn and cotton fields. To attract young workers, he built the Howell Graves Grammar School.

The city prepared for the explosion of prosperity. The people came. The land investors bought every parcel of land they could find, some no more than 25-feet wide. The publicists poured in and produced promotional films that declared the dawning of a new age. The politicians passed a law that gave Henry Ford control of the dam and the mighty Tennessee River. Control of the waterway was the vital and last piece of the puzzle to fall into place. Everything was set. The dream was in the making. The vision was forecast until President Woodrow Wilson vetoed the bill. With one swipe of the pen, the dream was gone!

Speculators mourned over one high priced and now worthless property. One can visit Muscle Shoals today and find some of the most beautiful corn and cotton fields side-walked, guttered, and curbed as silent symbols of a dream that is no more. The Howell Graves Grammar School houses the Muscle Shoals Board of Education.

ONE MINUTE MESSAGE: Only God can resurrect our dreams.

Story Ends

Revelation 21:1-7

A pastor took his small daughter to see a matinee performance of *Snow White*. The audience was full of little children and everyone was happy until the evil witch appeared. She seemed to be having her way, and the children began to get disturbed. Some children began to cry. Finally, the pastor's little girl got up on the edge of her seat and exclaimed, "Wait a minute! Wait a minute! I know this story — my mommy has read me this story many times. It comes out okay in the end. You don't have to be afraid."

ONE MINUTE MESSAGE: God knows how the story ends. So do we!

Index

Gotta Minute

About The Author

Gary L. Carver recently retired after over fifty years in the pastorate, serving Churches in Indiana, Alabama, and Tennessee, the last two of which were the First Baptist Church of Chattanooga, Tennessee, and the First Cumberland Presbyterian Church, also of Chattanooga, Tennessee. Carver is a graduate of Samford University (B.A.) and the Southern Baptist Theological Seminary (M.Div. and D.Min.) He has done additional study at the Candler School of Theology with Fred B. Craddock and received the Charles E. Merrill Fellowship to study at Harvard with Harvey Cox. In 1986, Carver received the Freedom's Foundation at Valley Forge's Principal Award for Public Address. He also is the author of *Out From the Ordinary*, *Acting on the Absurd*, *Distinctively Different*, *Search for Serendipity*, *Living A Victorious Life*, with Tom Garrison and *Stories That Live, The Parables of Jesus*.

For over 35 years, his radio spot "Gotta Minute?" has run almost continuously.

CPSIA information can be obtained
at www.ICGtesting.com
Printed in the USA
BVHW030205020821
613403BV00013B/195

9 780788 029608